A MYSTERY IN THE CLOUDS

Thank you to our first readers:
Maximiliano Abril Vanegas (8)
Sofía Grace Aragon Bayro (11)
Laura Bayless Velásquez (8)
Sara Bayless Velásquez (10)
Talia Cavassa de la Puente (9)
Matías de la Puente Velásquez (9)
Nicolás de la Puente Velásquez (6)
Vera Vilela Varillas (10)
Vicente Vilela Varillas (11)

MACHU PICCHU: A MYSTERY IN THE CLOUDS

Editor-in-Chief: Adriana Roca
Graphic and Creative Direction: Raquel Tudela
Graphic Direction and Design: Book and Play Studio – BaPstudio.co
Oscar Adolfo Abril Ortiz / Alejandro Amaya
Illustrations and Colorization: Nathaniel Rueda, Tamie Tokuda, Camilo José Rivera and Camilo Ulloa
Style Editor: Jorge Cornejo Calle
Translation: Laura Healy
Copyediting: Maria Fe Carranza

Edited by
Ediciones Pichoncito S. A. C.
Jr. Santa Rosa 359, Barranco
Lima, Peru
www.pichoncito.pe
R. U. C. 20603234643
First Edition in English: May 2025

Print run: 3,000
Printed by
Corporate Graphics Commercial
1750 Northway Drive
North Mankato, MN 56003
United States

May 2025
ISBN: 978-612-4450-59-4
Legal deposit at the National
Library of Peru n.° 2024-12599

Machu Picchu

A MYSTERY IN THE CLOUDS

SERGIO VILELA GALVÁN
JOSÉ CARLOS DE LA PUENTE
ILLUSTRATED BY BOOK AND PLAY STUDIO

This is a story woven from bits and pieces of reality. It is a tale for children, but we didn't make it up. Everything you are about to read was painstakingly written by two storytellers who picked out the most exciting and surprising details from the latest research on the Incas to help transport you back in time. We've worked together to explain all of Machu Picchu's secrets to you.

Each sentence and each illustration contains the voices and the patient work of researchers from all over the world (historians, archaeologists, engineers, and journalists) who have spent years figuring out what daily life was like in the time of the Incas: who they were, what they ate, how they dressed, what they thought about and why they built Machu Picchu. How do they know? Every detail counts: an old manuscript, a map, a wall, a piece of clothing, a tool, bones, teeth or leftover food. When put under the microscope, things reveal their secrets.

In addition to reading and hearing this story of Machu Picchu, we wanted you to be able to see it. On these pages, you'll find images that no one has ever seen but that we've tried many times to imagine: what the mountains were like before the Incas built Machu Picchu on top of them, what it looked like when thousands of people were carving and moving the enormous stone blocks, or how they got water to the citadel. A team of talented graphic artists has used the available artefacts and images, some of which are hundreds of years old, to create illustrations that also incorporate what we now know about the Incas and Machu Picchu.

We'd like to dedicate this book to all children who've dreamed of learning about the Incas' citadel and also to those who know about it already, like Vicente (11), Vera (10), Matías (9) and Nicolás (6), who inspire us every day. We hope you'll enjoy this true story as much as they have.

SERGIO VILELA GALVÁN
JOSÉ CARLOS DE LA PUENTE

A JOURNEY THROUGH THE HISTORY OF MACHU PICCHU

Before we begin, we'd like to share the most important moments in this story. Think of this timeline as a map or compass that you can carry with you as you journey into the past and come across all the many things you're about to discover.

1200

The Incas have become a powerful kingdom and have started to expand from Cuzco into the southern Andes. They are fearsome warriors and great builders, constructing roads to connect different peoples under their control. **Quipus** are the technology that makes it possible for them to organize their burgeoning empire.

1430

Pachacuti is an Incan leader admired for his great ability to transform arid land into agricultural fields, rocky peaks into stone cities in the clouds, and natural springs into water fountains for the community. To do this, he mobilizes thousands of people under his command.

1440

The construction of Machu Picchu has begun, and thousands of men and women arrive from different parts of the empire to move tons of earth and enormous rocks, clearing the area where, for decades, they will work to build the citadel's terraces, walls, and temples.

1527

The Inca Huayna Capac dies. His sons, Huascar and Atahualpa, start fighting because both wish to become the new ruler and take over their father's control and leadership of Tahuantinsuyo. This triggers a civil war that divides the empire and makes it vulnerable to the enemies who have arrived from across the ocean.

1532

Francisco Pizarro arrives in Cajamarca with a conquering army of fewer than two hundred men. He begins to organize an alliance between the Spanish and the Incas' ancient enemies. This joint force captures Atahualpa. Pizarro demands an ambitious ransom of silver and gold. Although he hauls in an incredible amount, he lets the execution of the Inca proceed.

1534

The Spanish conquistadores have benefited from their army's advantages: their **horsemen** and **swords** are extremely hard to beat. Cuzco falls into the hands of Francisco Pizarro, who takes control of the empire's capital. Tahuantinsuyo becomes the Governorate of New Castile and, soon after, the Viceroyalty of Peru.

1572

The last Incas have taken refuge in Vilcabamba for almost four decades. From there, they have tried to regain control of the empire. Pizarro and almost all the early conquistadores have died. The Spanish-Indigenous army manages to capture Vilcabamba and put an end to the city. The Incas are defeated after years of resistance.

1600–1800

Several families of farmers—who had been living in the area around Machu Picchu and had been forced to abandon it during **the conquest of Vilcabamba**—start returning to their old land. Some of them succeed, and, for the next two centuries, their heirs live in Machu Picchu and its surroundings. The citadel is never lost.

1824

The Spanish army surrenders to the patriot armies of **José de San Martín** and **Simón Bolívar**, who have joined forces to defeat them. Three years earlier, in a village north of Lima, San Martín had declared independence. The Republic of Peru is born, and the king of Spain admits defeat.

1902

Agustín Lizárraga lives at the foot of Machu Picchu, near the Vilcanota River. It will be another nine years before an American explorer arrives to "discover" the citadel. Lizárraga walks among the ruins of the Temple of the Three Windows and writes his name on the wall, a clue for future explorers.

1910

Genara Suárez de Nadal sells an enormous estate to the second richest man in Cuzco, **Mariano Ignacio Ferro**. It's so big that it takes nine days on horseback to get from one side to the other. Inside this great expanse are mountains, forests, streams, and dozens of Incan structures and roads, which all have a new owner.

1911

Hiram Bingham arrives at Machu Picchu for the first time. The citadel is hidden beneath trees and underbrush that have grown for centuries, so he isn't impressed by his discovery at first. He's surprised to find families living there and sees that someone has written their name on one of the walls. He jots it down in his notebook.

1913

After his first expedition, **Bingham realizes how important the citadel is** for understanding Incan history. He gathers more resources and dedicates himself to cleanup, excavation, and research. He convinces *National Geographic*, the most important scientific magazine of the time, to break the news of his enormous discovery. The whole world learns that Machu Picchu exists.

1921

Ever since Bingham gave it the name, the world has known Machu Picchu as **"The Lost City of the Incas."** In Peru, the book *Cuzco and Its Monuments: A Travel Guide* is published, and tourism surrounding the Incas is beginning to grow. Around this time, the photographer Martín Chambi takes his first photographs of the citadel, which are sent by tourists as postcards.

2007

An international contest seeks out the **New Seven Wonders of the World**. The organizers receive millions of votes from all around the globe. In Peru, thousands of people without electricity or internet, especially in the Cuzco region, come from all over looking for a computer where they can cast their votes for Machu Picchu. The citadel in the clouds makes the list.

More than five hundred years ago, the Incas forged an extraordinary civilization in the Andes Mountains of Peru. They controlled and oversaw an enormous territory encompassing towering mountains, snow-capped peaks, and lakes of the clearest water. They built their villages near rivers that cut through steep ravines surrounded by pastures where they and the many peoples they conquered grazed their llamas and alpacas. In the valleys, they grew hundreds of varieties of potato and maize (corn). Surrounded by those mountains, they formed the most extensive and powerful empire in the Americas. They called it "Tahuantinsuyo." In their language, Quechua, *tawa* means "four" and *suyo* means "region." Their world had four parts that converged in Cuzco, the great center of power.

Like those rivers, the Incan Empire also descended from the mountains into the plains and the coastal desert, where they discovered the riches of the Pacific Ocean. In the extreme east, they explored the Amazon rainforest, but they couldn't get very far because the jungle was so dense. High in the mountains, they sculpted cities of stone like Machu Picchu, the most famous and impressive, without even the help of steel or the wheel. How did they do it? This is the amazing history of that citadel, of the ingenuity of those men and women who dreamed it up and built it in a place that seemed impossible. It's also the story of how the jungle continued to hide it over centuries, until it became invisible, and of all the things that had to happen for it to be rediscovered.

The ancient chronicles tell us that sometime around 1450, the Inca Pachacuti sought to find an ideal location to build a magnificent citadel, perhaps the only one of its kind in the whole empire. His scouts traveled many miles on long journeys through the mountains to locate the perfect site. Pachacuti's empire included about ten million people and was extremely well connected by a network of thousands of miles of stone roads that united Tahuantinsuyo. They called it Qhapac Ñan or "royal road." One of these routes penetrated the jungle to the northeast of Cuzco, several days' walk from the capital, in the direction of Ollantaytambo, another great citadel.

Many legendary structures, like the Temple of the Sun in Cuzco, are attributed to Pachacuti, and he is also credited with great battles against the Chancas, their most fearsome rivals. Historians of the time tell of how he expanded the empire with his great army and mobilized thousands of men and women to transform mountains into cities of stone. The Incas believed their leader was the favorite child of the Sun and had the power to turn rocky ground into farmland to feed the whole population. Machu Picchu must have been a complex but fascinating project for Pachacuti as he continued to expand the empire. Incan engineers and architects had learned to build in a way that integrated their structures into the landscape. To do this, they had to be sure the chosen site combined three key elements.

THE **QHAPAQ ÑAN** OR "ROYAL ROAD" WAS MORE THAN 20,000 MILES LONG. IT ALLOWED THE INCAS TO

TRANSPORT FOOD AND GOODS FROM DIFFERENT ECOSYSTEMS AND REGIONS TO ALL OTHER PARTS OF THE EMPIRE

RECEIVE INFORMATION IN THE CAPITAL, CUZCO, FROM CITIES AS FAR AWAY AS QUITO IN ONLY TWELVE DAYS, BY WAY OF THE *CHASQUIS* OR INCAN MESSENGERS

EASILY MOBILIZE ARMIES THROUGHOUT THE ENTIRE KINGDOM TO MAINTAIN CONTROL

RELOCATE WORKERS RESPONSIBLE FOR CONSTRUCTION PROJECTS THROUGHOUT THE EMPIRE

Pachacuti and his engineers knew that their first and most important job was to make sure that each great building project had a natural water source nearby. "Let's find a place with a natural spring that we can channel toward the new city," must have been one of Pachacuti's first directions to those setting off to explore the mountains above the Vilcanota river, in the region of Antisuyo. Before they could start, they had to be sure they would have fresh water for drinking, bathing, and cooking. The Incas knew that springs of crystal clear water arose on some mountaintops, descending from the peaks into the ravines and valleys below. With that idea first in mind, they left Cuzco and set off on their quest.

The scouts who were sent ahead knew that the chosen site would also have to be near a granite quarry with enough material because so many stones would be needed to build the great citadel the Incas were imagining. Pachacuti and his ancestors had learned to build in places where they found lots of different kinds of rock and stone, which they could cut, sculpt, and polish to build houses, temples, and other buildings—rather than transporting them from far away. When they left Cuzco, the Inca must also have reminded his scouts of another thing that was equally important: "We'll know we've found the ideal spot when we find a site surrounded by great mountains." These were the protector gods, which the Incas called *apus*. And so they set off on many long treks.

Finally, the scouts found just the right spot: a sort of terrace between two mountains where they would build Machu Picchu. When they caught sight of that magnificent, endless horizon, the beauty of the landscape enchanted them. Looking out from Machu Picchu—which means "old mountain"—toward the mountain in front of them—which they would call "Huayna Picchu" or "young mountain"—they must have thanked the sun god for having guided them there. Though they never could have expected it, the ambitious project the Incas were about to begin would make them famous throughout the whole world centuries later.

Machu Picchu was in the mountains, though at a lower altitude than Cuzco. The Incas started planning a new road from the nearest point of access to the Qhapaq Ñan down to where the chosen site was located, where the Andes met the edge of the high jungle. Machu Picchu would be the entry point to this unexplored region of their territory—an area rich in resources like wood, feathers, and medicinal plants. The new citadel would be on the border of that world, which was still unknown to the Incas. From there, Pachacuti may have concluded, it would be easier to explore it and control it.

They set to work. Pachacuti had mobilized thousands of people, who arrived from different parts of the empire. The work would take many years and the combined force of many individuals. Men and women began the most difficult jobs. Some women made sure there was enough food and the agricultural fields were well tended. Others accompanied the most grueling tasks with music and song to keep the workers' spirits high. Even children, who had moved there with their parents, helped with tasks like hunting small birds. The Incas began construction using their typical style—transforming the mountains but respecting nature—so that Machu Picchu would blend seamlessly with the landscape.

So, in the great rocky and irregular space between those two mountains—the old and the young, which seemed to be looking at each other—they began building the citadel with enormous care. Their next most important job was also a great challenge, but a familiar one. The torrential rains, very common in that region between December and March, endangered their progress. While hundreds of workers were tasked with getting spring water to the site, others were figuring out how to divert the rainwater away. Pachacuti asked his best engineers to figure out how to do it. The Incas had spent years studying the destructive force of rain, but never before had they encountered the problem on such a grand scale. With the citadel's water supply guaranteed, the Incas now turned their attention to controlling it. Then, they got a great idea.

MACHU PICCHU IS A LITTLE MORE THAN 500 YEARS OLD. ITS **DRAINAGE SYSTEM** HAS WITHSTOOD MORE THAN 3,000 FEET OF RAIN SINCE ITS CONSTRUCTION.
MACHU PICCHU (8,766 FEET)
CENTRAL SQUARE
DISTANCE: 1,640 FEET
THE CITADEL IS SITUATED ON TOP OF THE **VILCABAMBA BATHOLITH**, A HUGE GRANITIC ROCK MASSIF OF VOLCANIC ORIGIN. THE WEIGHT OF THIS ENORMOUS ROCK ON TOP OF THE MOUNTAIN MAKES IT MORE RESISTANT TO EARTHQUAKES.

To start, they built stepped terraces, working from the bottom up. These platforms were like stone belts strapped around the mountain, tying it down. Very patiently, they filled each terrace, first with medium stones, then with smaller stones, and finally with a thick layer of dirt. This task alone took years. The terraces would be the visible surface of a system designed like a giant filter, which would help the structure better absorb the water that kept falling from the sky and threatened to destroy everything.

TERRACES OR **PLATFORMS** WERE MOSTLY USED BY THE INCAS AND OTHER GROUPS FOR GROWING FOOD. BECAUSE THEY WERE AT DIFFERENT ALTITUDES, IT WAS POSSIBLE TO TEST OUT HOW DIFFERENT PLANTS AND FRUITS WOULD GROW ON ONE LEVEL OR ANOTHER. THE TERRACES ACTED AS LABORATORIES.

With the terraces complete, they focused their effort on another part of the drainage network they'd started work on. This system directed water out onto their farmland and, from there, diverted the overflow to the Vilcanota River, which ran at the foot of the mountains. Though it seems unbelievable, all this work—the majority of what Machu Picchu's builders built—can't even be seen because it's all underground. More than half the time the Incan engineers spent on construction was allocated to protecting Machu Picchu from the six feet of rain that fell on it each year.

Then, starting halfway up the mountain, the builders created long rows of stepped terraces. When they reached the top, they did the same where the great plaza of the citadel would be. There, to complete the drainage system, they dug a ten-foot hole—as if they were building a giant swimming pool—and filled it up with pieces of rock that came from the carving and fitting of stone blocks at the site. Next, they added gravel and dirt. They would have needed an estimated three thousand people, men and women, working for months to make all of this possible. These foundations were put down across the width and breadth of an area the size of forty soccer fields. The work was titanic.

When they'd finished filling it back in, hiding all of their labor, they were able to safely continue building the citadel. To complete the rain protection system, they started building about one hundred twenty drainage canals throughout Machu Picchu. The canals began directing the flow of the rain: even today you can see how they work. They carry water from the highest points down to the terraces and central plaza, the areas best equipped to absorb and get rid of the most rain. The Incan engineers were able to come up with all this thanks to the time they'd spent observing nature and understanding its behavior.

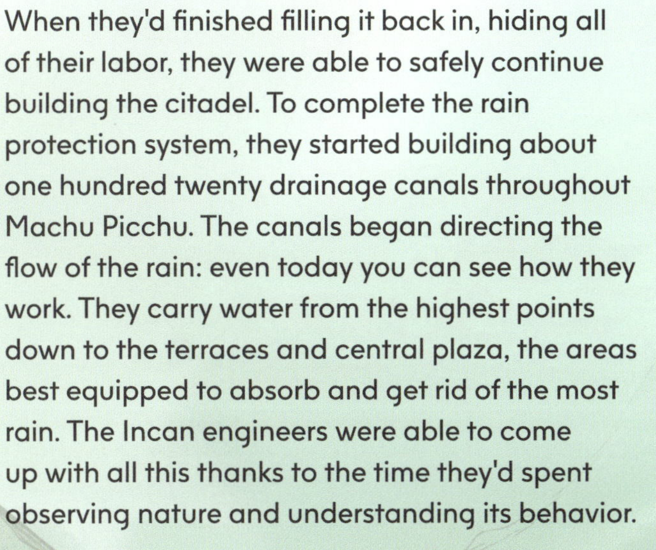

THE INCAS HAD **AN INCREDIBLE COMMAND OF WATER**. THE FINEST EXAMPLE OF THEIR HYDRAULIC KNOWLEDGE IS THE GROUP OF FOUNTAINS AT **TIPÓN**, LOCATED IN THE TOWN OF OROPESA, NEAR CUZCO. THERE, THEY WORSHIPED THE WATER, CHANNELING IT THROUGH CANALS AND FOUNTAINS JUST TO ADMIRE THE BEAUTY OF ITS MOVEMENT.

Pachacuti had summoned all his builders' ingenuity to protect Machu Picchu from the rain; now, the Inca turned his engineers' attention to the fresh water supply. Starting at the spring they'd found some seven hundred fifty yards away, the Incas created a long stone canal with a gradual slope or gradient to get the water all the way to the citadel.

Once in Machu Picchu, the water was channeled from the top down through a system of sixteen fountains, which builders installed in different parts of the citadel in order to reach every resident. By the time Machu Picchu was ready to welcome the Inca and his entourage decades later, the builders had made sure that there was enough water flowing through the city to supply about a thousand people without anyone being thirsty.

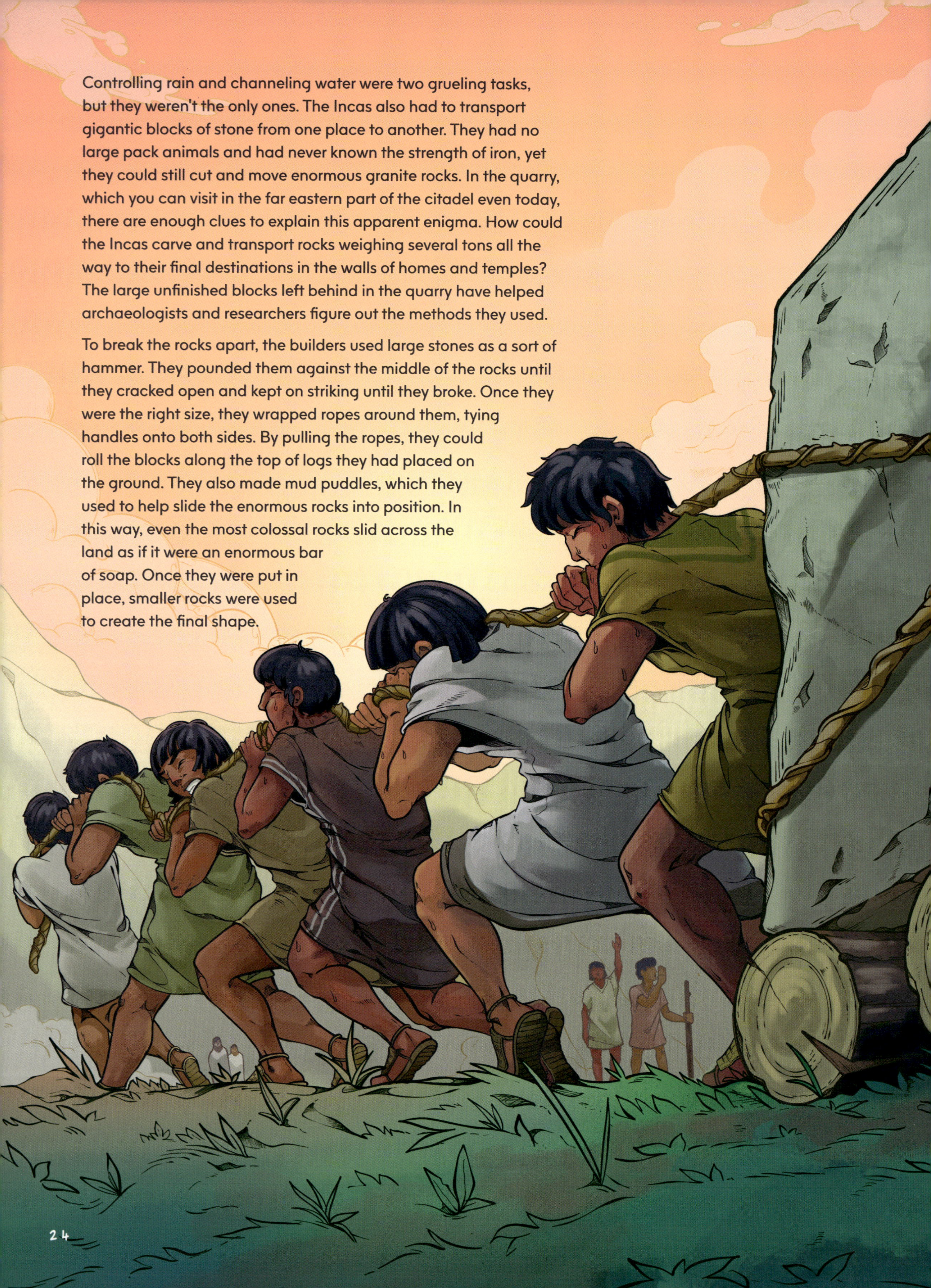

Controlling rain and channeling water were two grueling tasks, but they weren't the only ones. The Incas also had to transport gigantic blocks of stone from one place to another. They had no large pack animals and had never known the strength of iron, yet they could still cut and move enormous granite rocks. In the quarry, which you can visit in the far eastern part of the citadel even today, there are enough clues to explain this apparent enigma. How could the Incas carve and transport rocks weighing several tons all the way to their final destinations in the walls of homes and temples? The large unfinished blocks left behind in the quarry have helped archaeologists and researchers figure out the methods they used.

To break the rocks apart, the builders used large stones as a sort of hammer. They pounded them against the middle of the rocks until they cracked open and kept on striking until they broke. Once they were the right size, they wrapped ropes around them, tying handles onto both sides. By pulling the ropes, they could roll the blocks along the top of logs they had placed on the ground. They also made mud puddles, which they used to help slide the enormous rocks into position. In this way, even the most colossal rocks slid across the land as if it were an enormous bar of soap. Once they were put in place, smaller rocks were used to create the final shape.

ANOTHER WAY THE INCAS SPLIT LARGE ROCKS WAS BY TAKING ADVANTAGE OF NATURAL CRACKS IN THE STONE TO CREATE HOLES. THEY INSERTED THIN LOGS, POURED IN WATER, AND LET THEM SIT. OVER TIME, THE WATER EXPANDED THE WOOD OF THE LOGS, WHICH CAUSED THE ROCK TO SPLIT.

The great stones were placed one on top of the other to form walls, windows, and the beams over doorways. The ramps, once in place, were used throughout construction, with hundreds of workers pulling dozens of large rocks up their slopes. The rocks weren't completely carved when they brought them; even today, some still show outcroppings that were used to attach vines or to hold them up. When they were placed in their final position, builders used small taps to smooth the stones' surface, forming perfect blocks.

Very patiently and with the coordinated effort of hundreds of workers, the citadel was built over the course of thirty years. During that time, they overcame many challenges, like once when they found an enormous rock embedded right where they were supposed to build a temple. They decided to build it anyway, guided by the natural form of the landscape, without destroying the rock. At the foot of Huayna Picchu, they carved another big rock to match the silhouette of the mountain behind it. One temple even has a window that precisely frames the mountain across from it. The Incas observed their environment and incorporated it into the design.

But the citadel wasn't just a place to honor the gods or the great labor of the builders. Accompanied by their ancient kings and queens, whose bodies had been mummified, Machu Picchu's residents practiced rituals giving thanks for all the Sun, the Moon, and the Earth had offered them. The Incas were experts at reading the signs of nature; using what they'd learned from the stars and their rhythms and from the changing seasons, they knew the ideal times for planting and harvesting.

Incan priests and priestesses were mainly in charge of rituals at the citadel. Machu Picchu had several temples and places to observe the movement of the sun, the moon, and the stars. One of them was Intihuatana, a long angular block of stone that acted as a sundial. They got their bearings by reading the shadows that the sun projected on its base. As the day passed, Intihuatana's shadows would keep on moving, until the sun disappeared on the horizon.

THE INCAS WERE VERY CLEVER IN THE WAY THEY STUDIED THE STARS. AT NIGHT, INSTEAD OF LOOKING AT THE SKY, THEY LOOKED TO THE GROUND. THERE, THEY CARVED OUT ROCKS AND FILLED THEM WITH WATER, TURNING THEM INTO MIRRORS. THESE ROCKS WORKED LIKE A TELESCOPE.

Among the Incas, observing stars and planets and interpreting their signals was a job reserved for religious leaders, who performed the task from temples in the upper part of the citadel. The structure known today as "El Torreón" (The Turret) had little to do with defense. In fact, its fine semicircular wall is very similar to the one at Qoricancha, another temple, which was the most important ceremonial center in Cuzco and in the entire Incan Empire. That's why it's possible that this curved structure might have been the most sacred place in Machu Picchu, the perfect place to make contact with the gods and receive their messages.

The awe that Machu Picchu inspires has given way to all kinds of legends. Many visitors can't believe it was built by human beings. Everyone wonders—and some have trouble understanding—how rocks weighing several tons fit one on top of the other so precisely that not even a coin can fit between them. That's why there are always incredulous travelers who, instead of believing in the Incas' skill, think Machu Picchu must be the work of aliens or giants. They don't understand how the rocks could have gotten there from so far away. But the rocks were always nearby.

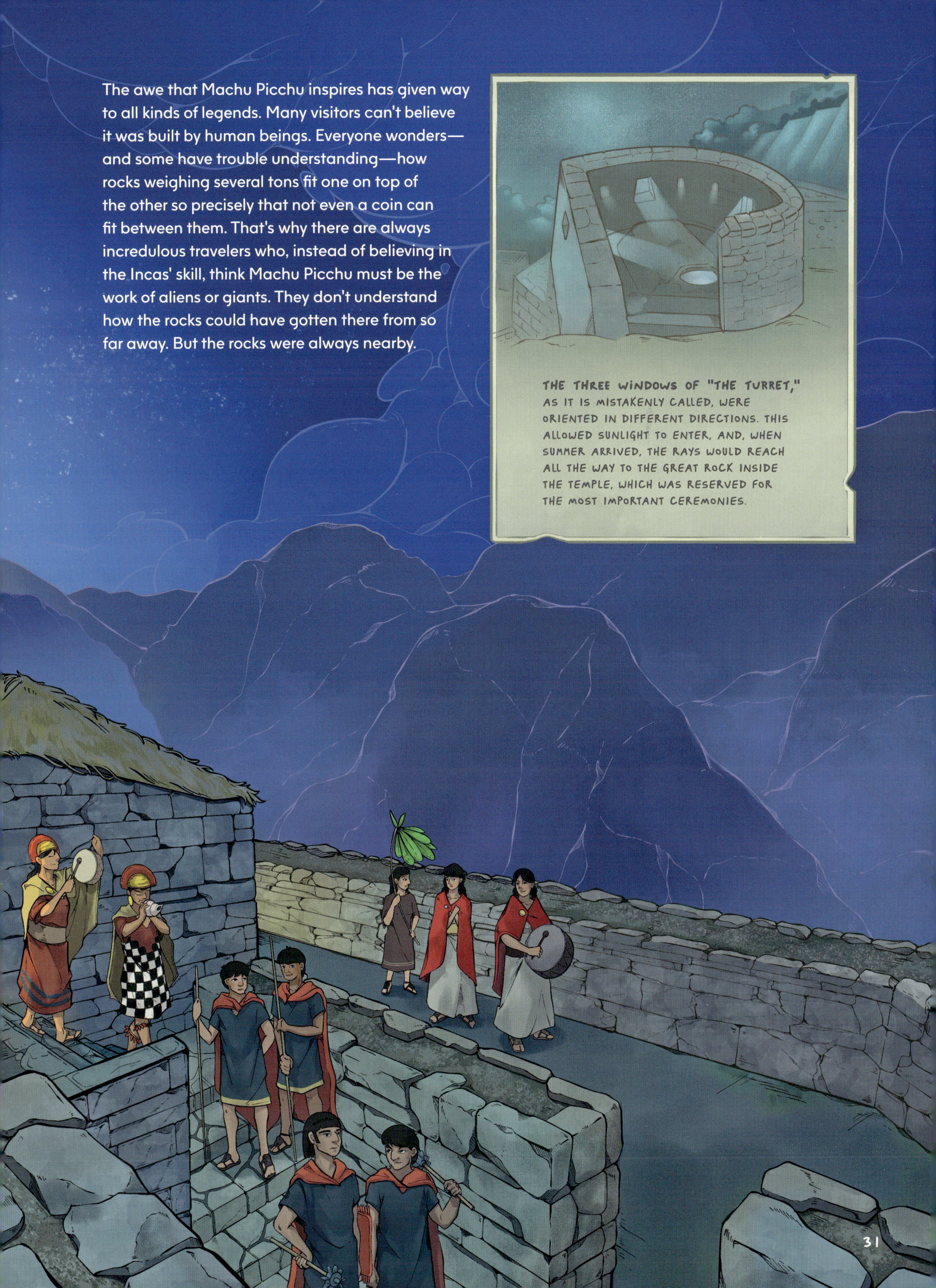

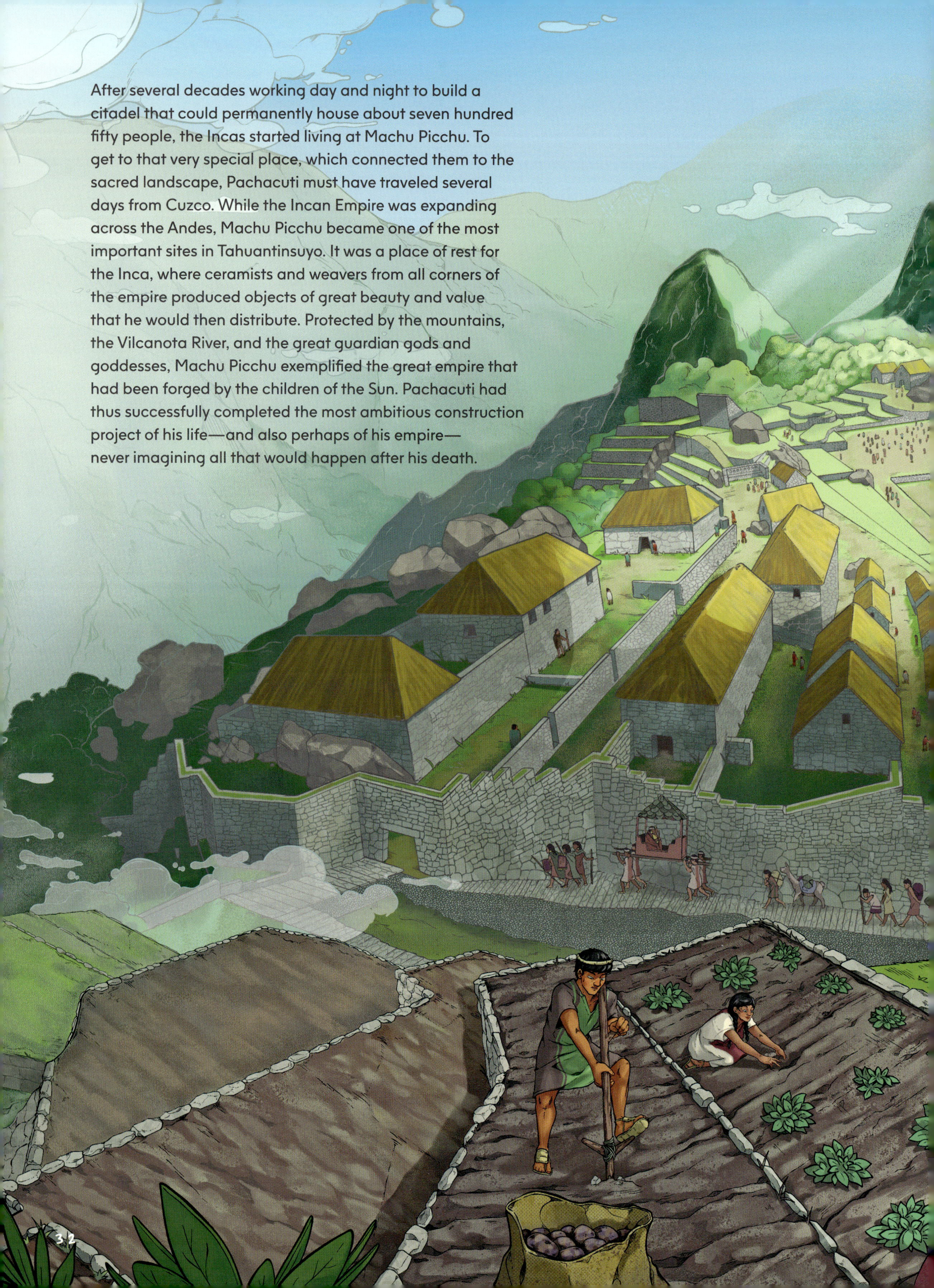

After several decades working day and night to build a citadel that could permanently house about seven hundred fifty people, the Incas started living at Machu Picchu. To get to that very special place, which connected them to the sacred landscape, Pachacuti must have traveled several days from Cuzco. While the Incan Empire was expanding across the Andes, Machu Picchu became one of the most important sites in Tahuantinsuyo. It was a place of rest for the Inca, where ceramists and weavers from all corners of the empire produced objects of great beauty and value that he would then distribute. Protected by the mountains, the Vilcanota River, and the great guardian gods and goddesses, Machu Picchu exemplified the great empire that had been forged by the children of the Sun. Pachacuti had thus successfully completed the most ambitious construction project of his life—and also perhaps of his empire—never imagining all that would happen after his death.

Years later, Pachacuti's heirs began to hear rumors of strange men arriving by sea on enormous rafts. These men—with their pale skin, long beards, and metal clothing—were Spanish explorers. Led by a man named Francisco Pizarro, they had traveled for months with the sole purpose of conquering the Incan empire. It was 1532, and their expedition in search of gold, silver, and other riches had advanced into Peruvian territory. At that time, the kingdom was engaged in a power struggle between two brothers named Huascar and Atahualpa, sons of the Inca Huayna Capac, who had recently died. The war had divided Tahuantinsuyo: Atahualpa ruled the north from Quito and Cajamarca, and Huascar defended the south and the capital, Cuzco.

The confrontation between the brothers gave Pizarro and his men a one-of-a-kind chance to carry out their plans. There were only a few conquistadores, but their weapons roared like thunder, their horses seemed invincible, their swords shined indestructible, and their words—written on paper—traveled long distances. Pizarro soon came to realize that many of the ethnic groups across the empire, who had been conquered by the Incas in the past, were willing to help defeat their old enemies. The foreigners' power had impressed them. So Pizarro and his men, at first a small army of fewer than two-hundred armed conquistadores, gained thousands of warrior allies and enough resources to take control of the entire Incan Empire.

The Incas were left with no choice but to relinquish control of their fortresses, towns, and cities—except for one. They withdrew into the dense jungle, about thirty miles from Machu Picchu, to a stronghold called Vilcabamba, "sacred plain." From there, for more than thirty years, the Incas fought their enemy. They planned multiple attacks to retake control of the empire, but they were unsuccessful. The Spanish tried to offer them a way out, but, in the end, they invaded Vilcabamba and finished off the last Inca, Tupac Amaru. Pizarro didn't live to see this historic defeat.

Machu Picchu had been abandoned by the Inca and the empire's prominent families ever since the Spanish conquistadores and their indigenous allies took over Cuzco. But other families who farmed the citadel's land stayed in the area. Although the Spanish built a city not far from there, they seem to have been unconcerned with Machu Picchu's existence. It stayed almost intact, tucked away in the middle of the Andes. Nourished by the rain, a green blanket of plants and trees grew and grew until its buildings were almost completely devoured.

Centuries later, in 1911, an American explorer who had seen and heard fascinating stories about Vilcabamba arrived in Peru. He was determined to find the city where the Incas had taken refuge after the Spanish arrived. The explorer, Hiram Bingham, had been born in Hawaii, a place famous for its beaches, its perfect surfing waves, and its restless volcanoes. As a boy, he had gone with his father on long treks through the mountains outside of Honolulu, where they lived. On those hikes with his dad, Hiram had developed a passion for expeditions, a passion that would carry him off to remote and astonishing places.

And so, after graduating from the prestigious Yale University, he decided to embark on an adventure in the faraway Andes Mountains of Peru. Hiram had also read about the snow-capped Coropuna, one of the tallest mountains in South America, and he wished to be the first foreigner to reach its peak. He could see himself planting his country's flag after days and days of impossible hiking. He convinced his college friends to help make this dream come true, and they supported him by raising money to pay for his first voyage. He wouldn't be traveling alone: other researchers were excited to follow him to Peru in search of the Incas' final refuge.

On the morning of May 5, 1911, Hiram left the Port of New York for Peru. He was accompanied by six people, including a plant-and-animal specialist, an expert in maps, a doctor, and an engineer. He brought some notebooks, a pair of tall boots, and the very latest Kodak cameras. The boat trip lasted several weeks. At the time, he never could have imagined that this expedition would change his life forever and that he was just a few days away from making Machu Picchu world famous.

When Bingham arrived in Peru, he found that another explorer, Annie Peck, had already climbed Coropuna. He quickly gave up on that idea and focused instead on his other plan: finding Vilcabamba, the city about which he had read so many exciting stories. So much time had passed, he had read, that—despite its significance to Incan history—no one knew where it was. This mystery convinced him that there must be a "lost city." His mission was to find it.

WOMEN'S RIGHT TO VOTE
HUAYNA PICCHU 8,835 FEET
COROPUNA 20,922 FEET
HUASCARÁN 22,237 FEET
WHEN SHE ARRIVED AT THE PEAK OF COROPUNA, **ANNIE SMITH PECK RAISED A FLAG PROMOTING WOMEN'S RIGHT TO VOTE.** SHE WAS SIXTY-ONE YEARS OLD. ONE YEAR BEFORE, AFTER FIVE ATTEMPTS, SHE HAD REACHED THE SUMMIT OF HUASCARÁN, ONE OF THE TALLEST PEAKS ON THE CONTINENT. ANNIE ALSO SCALED EXTREMELY HIGH MOUNTAINS IN MEXICO, AUSTRIA, BOLIVIA, AND SWITZERLAND. SHE WROTE SEVERAL BOOKS AND WAS ONE OF THE FIRST WOMEN TO TEACH LATIN AT A UNIVERSITY.

But he wasn't the first to go searching for Vilcabamba—other travelers had tried without luck. Bingham knew that Huascar and Atahualpa's younger brother, Manco Inca, had planned to counterattack and retake Cuzco from Vilcabamba. But the exact location of the legendary city, which had been lost in the mountains for centuries, was an enigma that would become the explorer's obsession. He looked for clues, consulted old maps, and spoke with travelers and Inca scholars who gave him more ideas. With all that information, his expedition in search of the lost city began to take shape.

In Lima, before traveling to Cuzco, Bingham met a curious researcher and librarian who was a treasure trove of valuable information. Carlos Romero was a lover of history and books. Though he'd gone a little deaf with age, they immediately understood each other well. Romero described the route Bingham should take to penetrate the dense jungle of Cuzco. "In the past, explorers have always gone the wrong way in search of the Incan ruins," Romero said. "You should follow the course of the river and climb up the western side of the mountains." That would be the key.

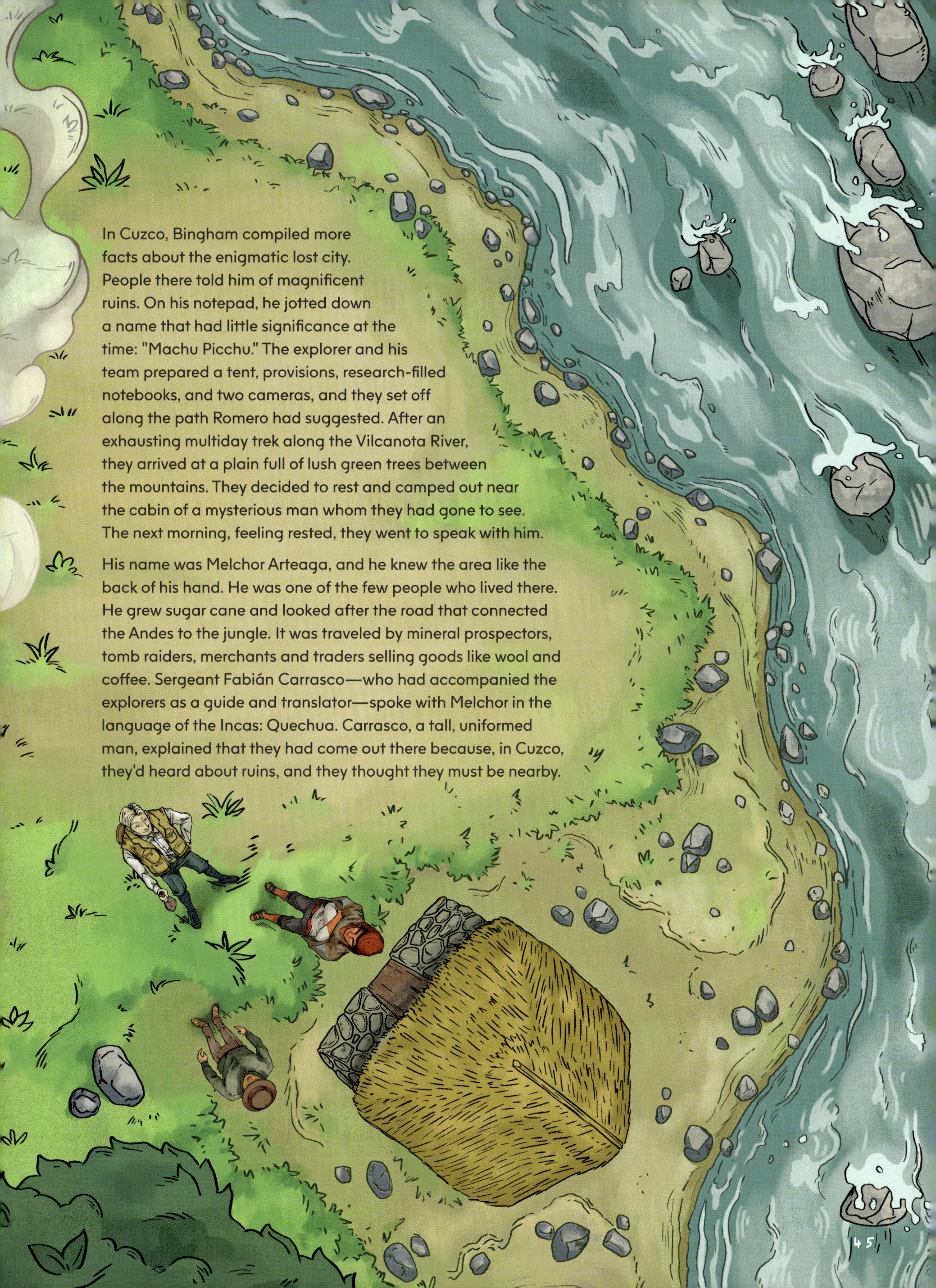

In Cuzco, Bingham compiled more facts about the enigmatic lost city. People there told him of magnificent ruins. On his notepad, he jotted down a name that had little significance at the time: "Machu Picchu." The explorer and his team prepared a tent, provisions, research-filled notebooks, and two cameras, and they set off along the path Romero had suggested. After an exhausting multiday trek along the Vilcanota River, they arrived at a plain full of lush green trees between the mountains. They decided to rest and camped out near the cabin of a mysterious man whom they had gone to see. The next morning, feeling rested, they went to speak with him.

His name was Melchor Arteaga, and he knew the area like the back of his hand. He was one of the few people who lived there. He grew sugar cane and looked after the road that connected the Andes to the jungle. It was traveled by mineral prospectors, tomb raiders, merchants and traders selling goods like wool and coffee. Sergeant Fabián Carrasco—who had accompanied the explorers as a guide and translator—spoke with Melchor in the language of the Incas: Quechua. Carrasco, a tall, uniformed man, explained that they had come out there because, in Cuzco, they'd heard about ruins, and they thought they must be nearby.

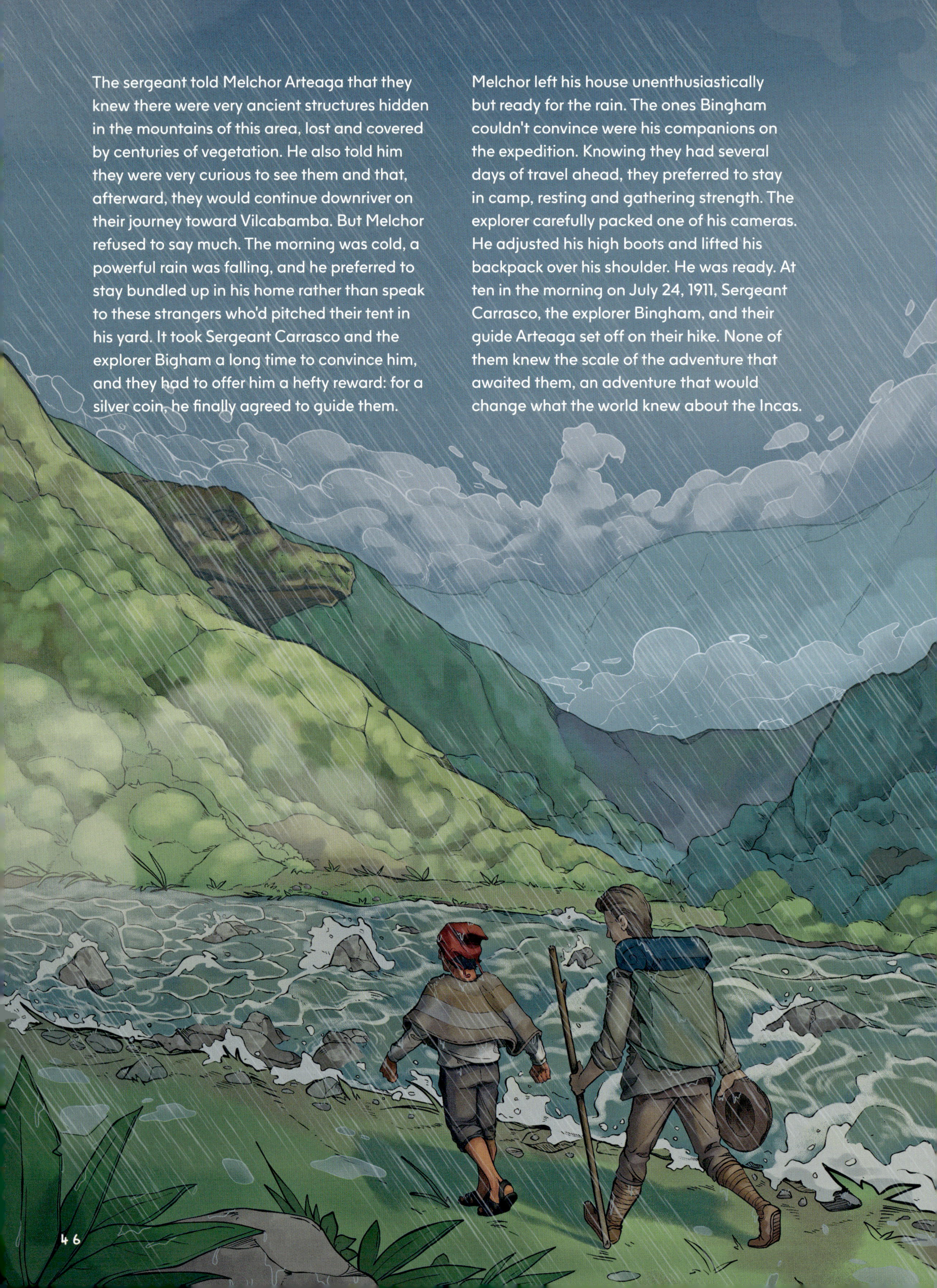

The sergeant told Melchor Arteaga that they knew there were very ancient structures hidden in the mountains of this area, lost and covered by centuries of vegetation. He also told him they were very curious to see them and that, afterward, they would continue downriver on their journey toward Vilcabamba. But Melchor refused to say much. The morning was cold, a powerful rain was falling, and he preferred to stay bundled up in his home rather than speak to these strangers who'd pitched their tent in his yard. It took Sergeant Carrasco and the explorer Bigham a long time to convince him, and they had to offer him a hefty reward: for a silver coin, he finally agreed to guide them.

Melchor left his house unenthusiastically but ready for the rain. The ones Bingham couldn't convince were his companions on the expedition. Knowing they had several days of travel ahead, they preferred to stay in camp, resting and gathering strength. The explorer carefully packed one of his cameras. He adjusted his high boots and lifted his backpack over his shoulder. He was ready. At ten in the morning on July 24, 1911, Sergeant Carrasco, the explorer Bingham, and their guide Arteaga set off on their hike. None of them knew the scale of the adventure that awaited them, an adventure that would change what the world knew about the Incas.

The path was wet. The members of the expedition had to be very careful not to slip and fall into the river that passed, loud and mighty, between steep walls of rock. They walked almost an hour. Then, Arteaga left the main trail and crossed through shrubs and trees to get to the very edge of the river. Someone had placed logs there and had tied them together with ropes to make a crossing to the other side. That improvised bridge over the Vilcanota seemed to be made of paper. Bigham asked if there might be another, safer route. But there was no other choice.

One by one, the travelers held their breath and shuffled inch by inch across the bridge like agile cats. On top of them, the rain came down with all its force; beneath them, the river roared menacingly. They arrived at the other shore. Melchor pointed out the tracks of the only route up the mountain. It looked slippery. They started climbing, being very careful to avoid the vipers that hid among the roots. As they went on, Bingham found some planks of wood placed like stairs. A little further, he saw a viper that had been stomped to death. His suspicion was confirmed: others had traveled this path.

They climbed however they could. Bingham grasped onto branches, trying not to glance down at the river, which looked smaller and smaller. The three travelers had to focus on each footstep because, by that point, their boots had filled with mud. They continued to climb, getting more and more exhausted. Time passed, and the stone structures Bingham had hoped to find did not appear. He started losing hope. Almost two hours had gone by since they had left camp. But there was no trace of the Incas. Around noon, they made it to the top of the mountain and took a break.

While his companions caught their breath, Bingham got up and went on. Just then, there appeared one, two, five, twenty stepped terraces, all very well-maintained, as if someone had been using them. Bingham stopped to observe and noticed one of them had a cornfield on top. *What's all this doing here?* he asked himself. He went on a few feet and suddenly found himself "confronted with the walls of ruined houses built of the finest quality of Inca stone work," as he would write in his diary about that captivating first impression. Although they were covered by vegetation, he could make out the shapes of dozens of structures. "It truly took my breath away." He was seeing Machu Picchu for the first time.

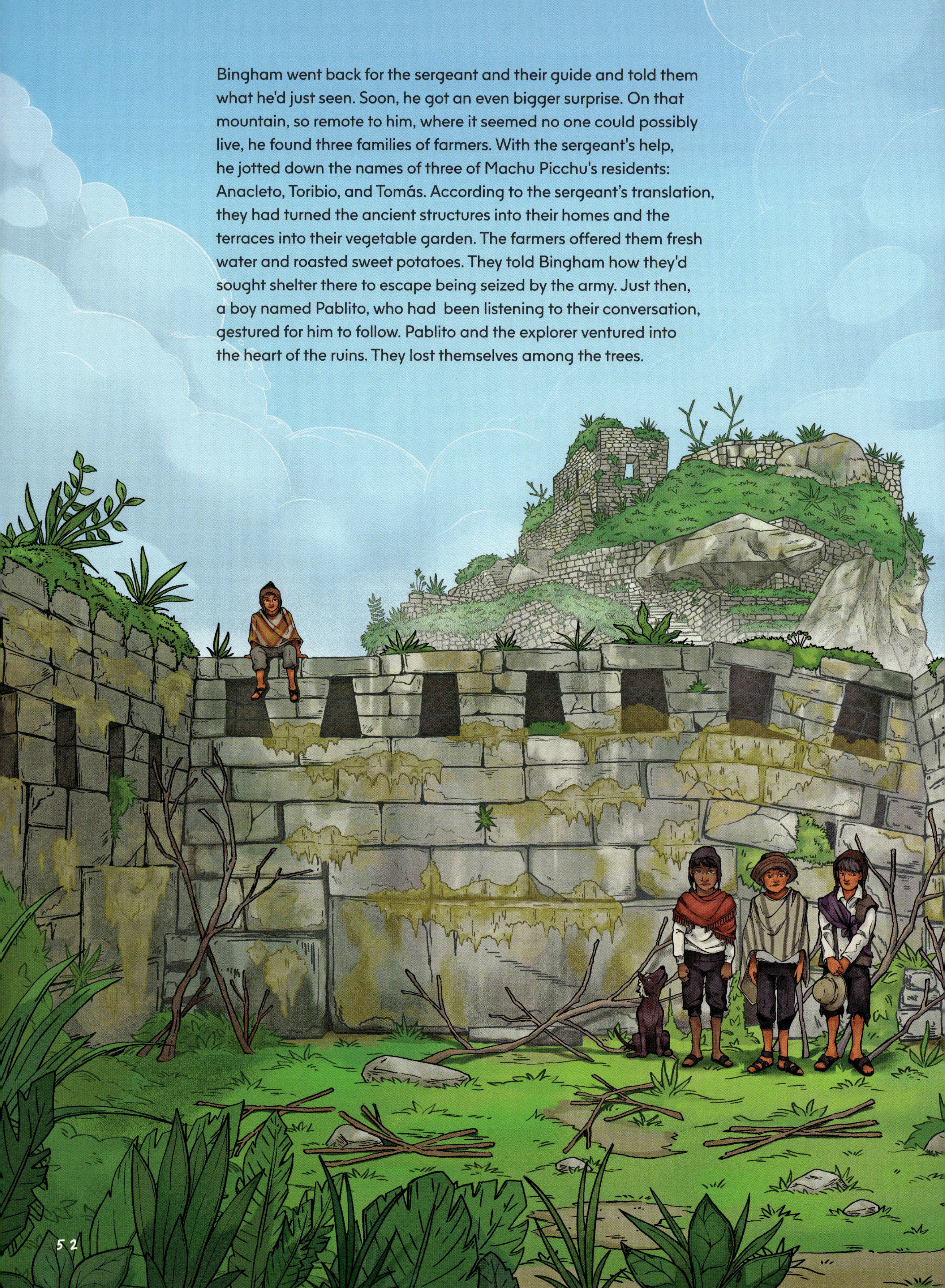

Bingham went back for the sergeant and their guide and told them what he'd just seen. Soon, he got an even bigger surprise. On that mountain, so remote to him, where it seemed no one could possibly live, he found three families of farmers. With the sergeant's help, he jotted down the names of three of Machu Picchu's residents: Anacleto, Toribio, and Tomás. According to the sergeant's translation, they had turned the ancient structures into their homes and the terraces into their vegetable garden. The farmers offered them fresh water and roasted sweet potatoes. They told Bingham how they'd sought shelter there to escape being seized by the army. Just then, a boy named Pablito, who had been listening to their conversation, gestured for him to follow. Pablito and the explorer ventured into the heart of the ruins. They lost themselves among the trees.

The farmers had lived there for years, isolated but protected from danger. But their estate on Machu Picchu wasn't free; they paid rent to a very rich family from Cuzco who owned the land. Bingham was beginning to better understand why they'd ended up here at the far edge of the Urubamba region and why they paid so little attention to the ruins around them. They were simply used to living alongside the roads, water canals, and stone walls built by the Incas, and they made use of them without a second thought. But for their visitor from so far away, all those structures peeking out were a treasure to be discovered. *Machu Picchu isn't lost anymore*, he thought. Now, everyone would know how to find the way there.

BINGHAM AND HIS TEAM TOOK MORE THAN 12,000 PHOTOGRAPHS. THE EXPEDITION'S CAMERAS, UNLIKE TODAY'S, HAD TO BE PLACED ON A TRIPOD, WHICH NEEDED TO BE PROPERLY LEVELED. THEN, THE ROLL OF FILM INSIDE THE CAMERA HAD TO BE VERY CAREFULLY EXPOSED TO THE LIGHT, CREATING NEGATIVES. BINGHAM RECOMMENDED TAKING SIX PRACTICE SHOTS BEFORE THE FINAL. AFTERWARDS, TO DEVELOP THE PHOTOGRAPHS, THE NEGATIVES WERE SUBMERGED IN A TANK OF HOT WATER AND DIFFERENT CHEMICALS. FINALLY, THEY HAD TO BE RINSED FOR SEVERAL MINUTES AND HUNG UP TO DRY BEFORE THEY WERE READY.

After exploring as much of the citadel as he could with Pablito, Bingham went back to the house of one of the farmers who'd first greeted them. After thanking them for the food and water, he and his companions, Sergeant Fabián Carrasco and their guide Melchor Arteaga, packed their things to head out. The next day, Bingham would need to get back on his route to search for the lost city of Vilcabamba. Before leaving, the explorer set up his camera on the stand he'd been lugging around and took the first panoramic photo of Machu Picchu. It would be the first image he'd show when he got home. Because of that image, the world would learn that there was a citadel amid clouds and mountains, a citadel that had been preserved for more than four-hundred years because it was so hard to get to.

Days later, Bingham and his team made it to Vilcabamba, where they found the remains of just a few stone structures. It was disappointing. Although they knew it had been the site of a great battle, Bingham thought it couldn't possibly be the famous lost city of the Incas. He convinced himself that Vilcabamba must be somewhere else, and he went back to his country with that idea in mind. His dream of finding that lost, wonderful, well-preserved city kept growing until he decided the "lost city" must be Machu Picchu instead. He was itching to get back to Peru. He organized a new expedition, this time with more resources and a research team, so they could clear roads, remove vegetation, and start figuring out how big the city really was and all the secrets it held about the Incas.

Bingham went back to Peru the following year, prepared to show the world the treasure he had found. His team worked long months. With the help of people in the Cuzco region who'd heard about his project and wanted to collaborate, they undertook history's greatest landscaping project. The owner of the property where the structures were located contributed provisions and sent some of his laborers to help. The Peruvian newspapers announced the discovery. As their work moved forward, Bingham came to understand that Machu Picchu, as it was called by the locals, wasn't just a handful of isolated structures. He had found a stone citadel, one in which many people must have lived.

Two years after his first visit, the work paid off. They had successfully cleaned up the citadel so all future visitors could discover its history. They found tools, containers, pieces of clothing, tombs with humans bones in them, and even some dog skeletons. All these clues helped researchers better understand what life had been like for the Incas. The first tourists also began to arrive. In 1913, Bingham and his team published the first photographs and descriptions of their discovery in the most important science magazine of the time, *National Geographic.* It was the first time the world had heard of Machu Picchu, and they saw it right there in the panoramic photo that would make it so popular.

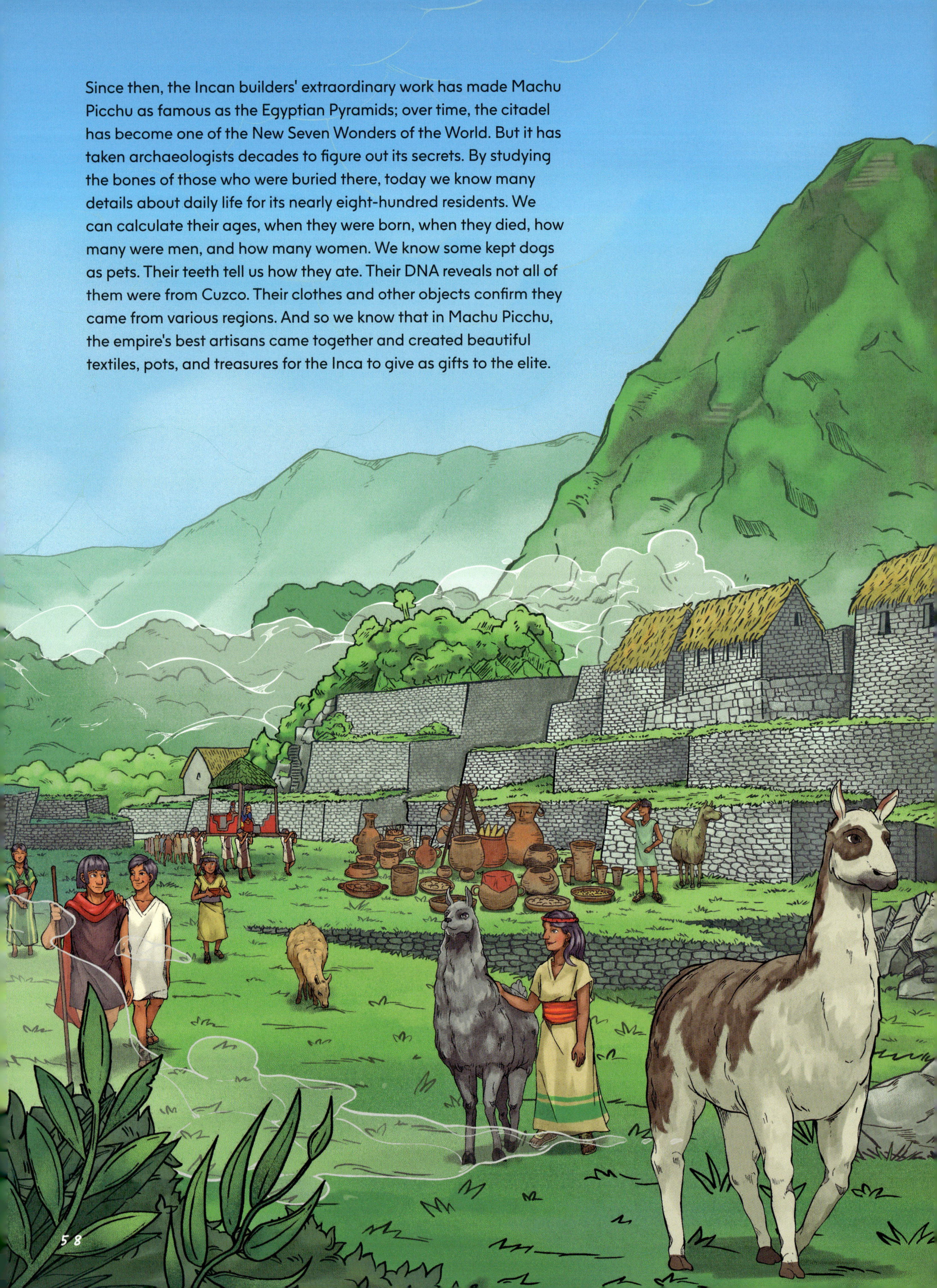

Since then, the Incan builders' extraordinary work has made Machu Picchu as famous as the Egyptian Pyramids; over time, the citadel has become one of the New Seven Wonders of the World. But it has taken archaeologists decades to figure out its secrets. By studying the bones of those who were buried there, today we know many details about daily life for its nearly eight-hundred residents. We can calculate their ages, when they were born, when they died, how many were men, and how many women. We know some kept dogs as pets. Their teeth tell us how they ate. Their DNA reveals not all of them were from Cuzco. Their clothes and other objects confirm they came from various regions. And so we know that in Machu Picchu, the empire's best artisans came together and created beautiful textiles, pots, and treasures for the Inca to give as gifts to the elite.

The men and women who've dedicated their lives to studying Machu Picchu have also revealed the ingenuity of the Incas' construction and how their advanced knowledge of engineering and architecture made it possible. We know not only when they built it but how. The care the Incas put into choosing the location of the temples and the precision with which they aligned their walls and windows to follow the movement of the sun, the moon, and the stars turned Machu Picchu into a giant observatory. It is a magical place that the Incas were forced to abandon when the Spanish arrived but that was able to maintain its connection to the past through families who, for centuries, went on living in the area. Despite a few people always having known these secret ruins existed, for most of us, the citadel vanished bit by bit into the mountains of Cuzco until the day it was rediscovered.

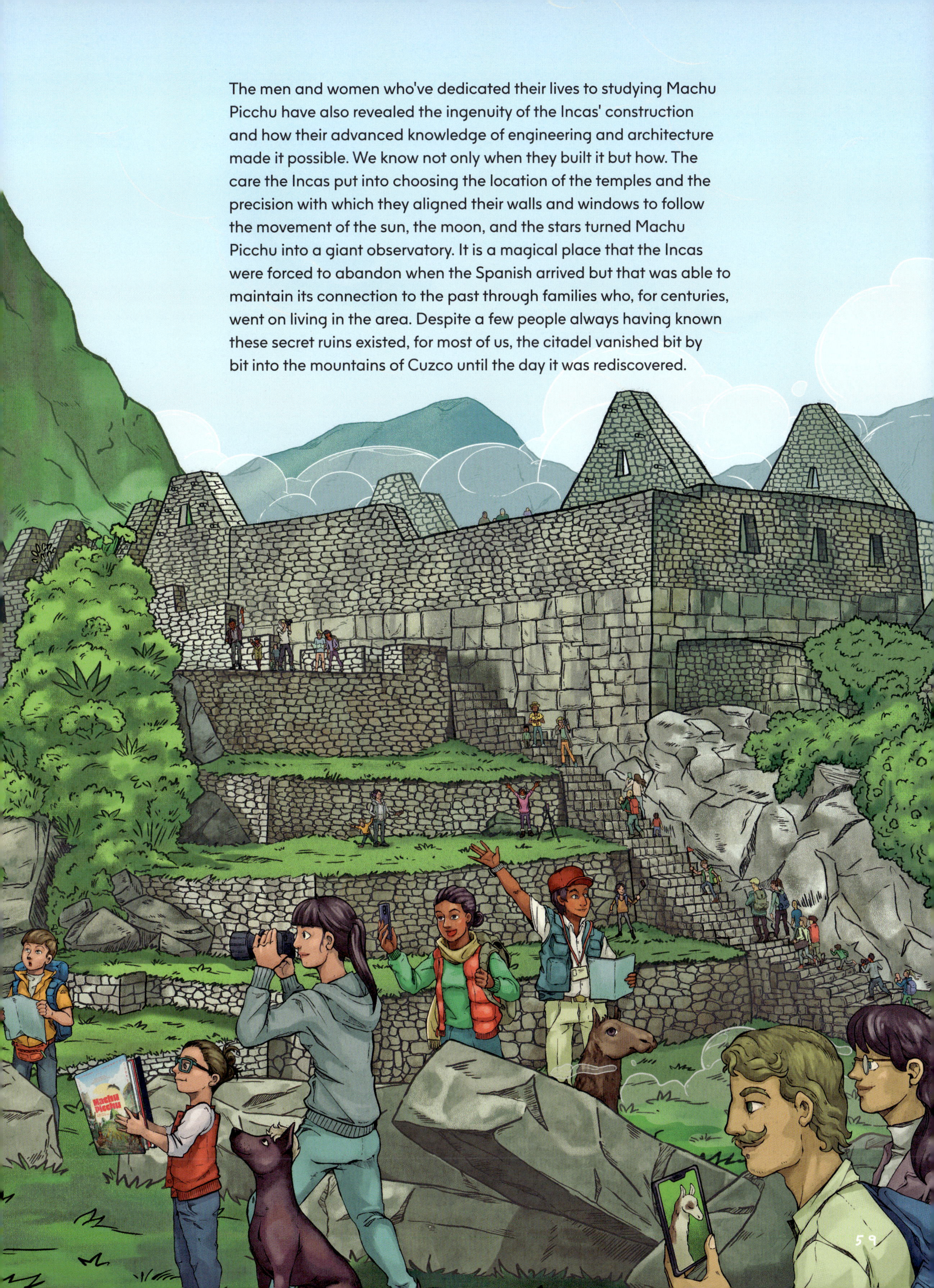

TEMPLE OF THE THREE WINDOWS
MAIN TEMPLE
SACRED SQUARE
SACRED AREA
INCA'S PALACE
TURRET
MAIN FOUNTAIN
ENTRANCE TO THE CITADEL
AGRICULTURAL SECTOR

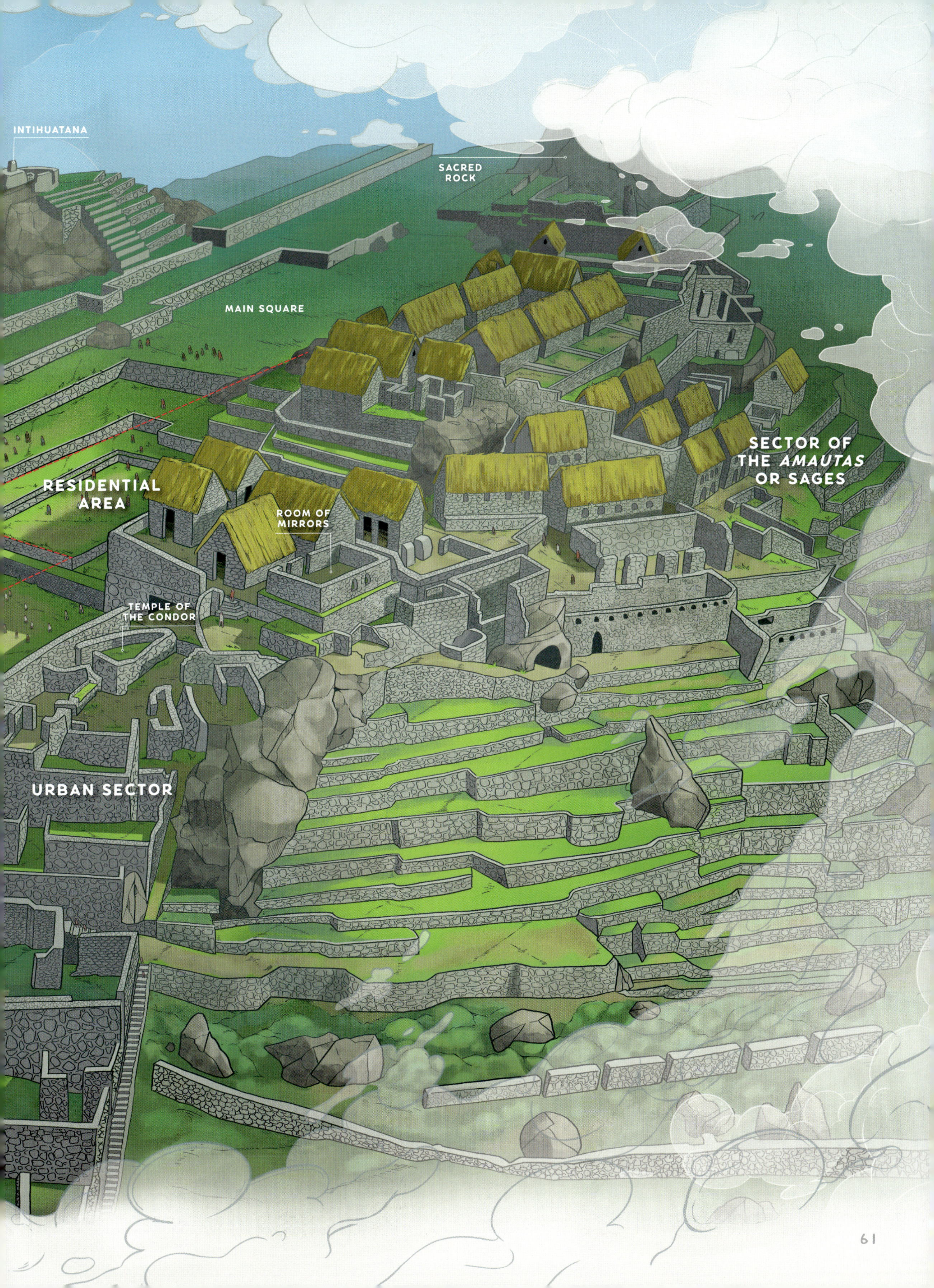
INTIHUATANA
SACRED ROCK
MAIN SQUARE
SECTOR OF THE *AMAUTAS* OR SAGES
RESIDENTIAL AREA
ROOM OF MIRRORS
TEMPLE OF THE CONDOR
URBAN SECTOR

We both visited Machu Picchu for the first time as kids, on different occasions and without knowing we would meet each other later in school. We were just a few years older than our own children are now, and, as it does for them, Machu Picchu left us wide-eyed and buzzing with a powerful and unsettling curiosity. Our parents and teachers had little to offer us at the time. There were no children's books about Machu Picchu anywhere, let alone one written for inquisitive minds. We never thought that we would become writers and certainly not that we would be the ones to write this story years later. In school, we memorized the famous list of fourteen Inca kings and some words—like *ayni*, *minka*, *ciudadela*, and Tahuantinsuyo—which made us feel closer to their bygone civilization. But back then, Machu Picchu and the Incas' fascinating universe were still shrouded in mystery. Ultimately, that first trip we took as child tourists led us here.

Years passed. One day, that lifelong curiosity about the Incas, along with an incredible article in the newspaper, brought us to work together. Since then, we've scoured many archives, interviewed dozens of people, and read hundreds of pages. A historian and a journalist, we navigated an ocean of information to unravel the complex ways in which we Peruvians relate to the most famous of all Incan sites. This work resulted in our book *Machu Picchu's Last Secret: Does the Incan Citadel Have an Owner* (*El último secreto de Machu Picchu. ¿Tiene dueño la ciudadela de los incas?*, Estruendomudo, 2018). The new book you have here is based on the research we did for that one; it's our attempt to provide the answers that our past selves couldn't find, in the form of a story.

This book would not have been possible without the enthusiasm and conviction of our editor, Adriana Roca, who supported this project from the very beginning. We'd also like to express our gratitude to the excellent team at Pichoncito, in particular Raquel Tudela, for embracing this idea and letting it take flight. We owe equal thanks to the limitless patience and creativity of the Book and Play team—with Oscar Abril and Alejandro Amaya at the helm—who made this book come alive in more than just words. In line and in color, Nathaniel Rueda, Tamie Tokuda, Camilo Rivera, and Camilo Ulloa formed an unbeatable design team. We also thank our families, especially Lynda and Jenny, for the time we stole away from them. Our first readers, both children and adults, guided us on this journey. To all of them, with whom we alternated roles as captain and crew on this ship as we steered safely into port, our most sincere thanks now that we can finally say: Land ho!

JOSÉ CARLOS DE LA PUENTE
SERGIO VILELA GALVÁN

FURTHER READING

An excellent starting point for young readers who want to learn more about the world of Machu Picchu's builders is *The Epic History of the Incas* (MALI/Pichoncito Flybooks, 2025). You can also consult *Los Peruguntones Incas*, by Andrea and Claudia Paz (Planeta, 2010). For those who wish to dig deeper into the myths and legends that helped form the world view of the Incas and other Andean residents in the time before the Spanish Conquest, see Maritza Villavicencio and Rubén Silva's book *Micaela conoce a Urpayhuachac. Un viaje por el Gran Camino Inca* (Ministerio de Cultura del Perú / Proyecto Qhapaq Ñan, 2019). The Virtual Library of the Peruvian Ministry of Culture (**https://repositorio.cultura.gob.pe/**) also has a variety of books on those themes, which can be downloaded for free, in the section "Libros para niños"/"Books for Children." María Rostworowski, one of the foremost specialists in Incan culture and society, has also published a series of stories about ancient Peru (Peisa/IEP, 2012-2013), which she recovered from chronicles that were written after the Conquest.

Older readers interested in exploring the works we used to research this book should refer to our previous book, *El último secreto de Machu Picchu. ¿Tiene dueño la ciudadela de los incas?* (Estruendomudo, 2018), which includes an extensive annotated bibliography. On the construction of Machu Picchu, we recommend the following works: Kenneth R. Wright and Alfredo Valencia Zegarra, *Machu Picchu: A Civil Engineering Marvel* (2000); Richard Burger and Lucy Salazar, *Machu Picchu: Unveiling the Mystery of the Incas* (2003); and Johan Reinhard, *Machu Picchu: Exploring an Ancient Sacred Center* (2007). We would also add two additional collections of academic essays for advanced readers: Fernando Astete and José M. Bastante, *Machu Picchu. Investigaciones interdisciplinarias* (2020) and Mariusz Ziółkowski, Nicola Masini, and José M. Bastante, *Machu Picchu in Context: Interdisciplinary Approaches to the Study of Human Past* (2022).

The best texts about the life and career of the explorer Hiram Bingham are the one written by his son Alfred M. Bingham, titled *Portrait of An Explorer: Hiram Bingham, Discoverer of Machu Picchu* (1989), and one by Christopher Heaney, titled *Cradle of Gold* (Palgrave Macmillan, 2010). More advanced readers can go directly to Bingham's own books, *Inca Land* (1922), *Machu Picchu: A Citadel of the Incas* (1930), and, above all, *Lost City of the Incas* (1948), which are available in many editions in English and Spanish.

PICHONCITO

THEIR GENERATION

THE WHO IN AMERICA 1967–69

THE WHO

THEIR GENERATION

THE WHO IN AMERICA 1967–69

PHOTOGRAPHS BY
TOM WRIGHT

WRITTEN BY
ANDY NEILL

FOREWORD BY
PETE TOWNSHEND

OMNIBUS PRESS
London / New York / Paris / Sydney / Copenhagen / Berlin / Madrid / Tokyo

(A division of the Wise Music Group
14–15 Berners Street, London, W1T 3LJ)

Cover and book design by Amazing15
Picture research by Andy Neill

ISBN 9781787601451

Every effort has been made to trace the copyright holders of the photographs in this book but one or two were unreachable. We would be grateful if the photographers concerned would contact us.

A catalogue record for this book is available from the British Library.

Printed and bound in India.

www.omnibuspress.com

CONTENTS

FOREWORD BY
PETE TOWNSHEND 8

01:
EALING ART BLUES 10

02: **1967**
I CAN SEE FOR MILES 18

03: **1968**
MAGIC BUS 96

04: **1969**
LISTENING TO YOU 156

EPILOGUE 174

ACKNOWLEDGEMENTS 176

FOREWORD BY PETE TOWNSHEND

Tom Wright's photos are a backroom boy's view of some of the most fun moments in Sixties' rock history. The Who, the Faces, the Stones.... he was around backstage with all of them. On the road sometimes with them too. Before all this he was a photography student at Ealing Art College where I too was an art student getting my brain fried and freed by the now legendary Roy Ascott. Tom introduced me to his vast vinyl collection of blues and rhythm and blues, and some oddities like Julie London. This was life changing for me. I feel sure I would have gotten around to discovering Jimmy Reed and Jimmy Smith and others in the end, but I was thrown a volley of great music that informed my playing and my writing and to some degree my philosophy of life.

Tom was a great friend to me, someone who spotted my innate talent and took me seriously. (I was a fairly geeky, silly kid when at art college.) I did have other friends who seemed to like me, but Tom was a formative ally, playing me records he knew would help me define a new style on guitar, and also indoctrinate me into the philosophy of the Blues – the downtrodden and forgotten, singing out their hearts to ease their sadness about life. It might seem extreme to compare life building a railroad, or picking cotton, with life in post-war England, but the message rang loud and clear: Whatever the blues, music would help to overcome. I decided to try to become a 'voice' for my disenfranchised generation.

Tom's photos capture moments that might at first sight seem not important enough to be celebrated, but it's their informality that makes them so special. I've lost count of the number of photos of the Who on stage, but there are very few of me posing in a field wearing a kaftan and Stetson, or sitting in a car with a whistle around my neck. He was a chronicler, with an eye for the passing moment, and it's a joy to be able to share all these passing moments with you all today...

Pete Townshend
London, 2024

01: EALING ART BLUES

It's not too far a stretch to assert that London's art colleges in the early Sixties served as important incubators for many a famous British rock musician. Keith Richards, Ron Wood, Eric Clapton, Jeff Beck, Jimmy Page, Ray Davies, David Bowie and Syd Barrett are some of the names that entered art institutes around the capital during this time, while honing their craft on the side. Ealing Technical College & School of Art, situated on St Mary's Road in the leafy west London borough of Ealing, was a prime example. In 1961, 16-year-old local resident and budding guitarist Pete Townshend started a two-year ground course there in graphic design.

PETE TOWNSHEND: I was going to Ealing as a summer student, and I got my entrance exam that way. Then when I started the course, it wasn't about art at all, it was all about cybernetics and communications with [British artist] Roy Ascott.

Ascott's revolutionary approach was to dispense with preconceived notions of what art (and life) should be about. Richard Barnes – known to all as Barney – who was an Ealing student at the same time and became a lifelong friend of Pete's, wrote in his Who biography *Maximum R&B*: "There is no doubt that confusing as the course appeared and, to a certain extent, was, it was the most exciting and aware and radical at that time." As well as improving his social skills, Pete's horizons were broadened by the bohemian, non-conformist atmosphere so prevalent at art college. There were important and often controversial lectures and displays given by jazz musicians, film writers, and artists such as Peter Blake (whose pop art symbolism utilised targets and badges – later so effectively adopted by the Who), Larry Rivers, Robert Brownjohn and radical playwright David Mercer. Some lessons were spent simply listening to jazz or classical music.

Outside his studies Pete pursued his musical aspirations in a local semi-pro group, the Detours, featuring singer Roger Daltrey and bass guitarist John Entwistle, both of whom he knew from attending Acton County Grammar School.

PETE TOWNSHEND: I kept my band work pretty secret at art college because it felt to me to be inestimably uncool, which I suppose it was in a way because we used to play Shadows and Beatles covers, Top 20 hits, and wear silly outfits as everybody did in those days. A few people knew about what I did but not many. There were several good musicians at art school. Most of them were jazz players – one was really brilliant at Chet Atkins' music – but I was learning to play country blues. One day this guy I knew, Tim Bartlett, whose younger brother Nick was one of my best friends, heard me playing a Snooks Eaglin song on acoustic guitar. He went rushing out to find his friend Tom Wright and brought him in. Tom heard me playing, and started to spread this story that I was some kind of a genius.

Tom Wright was born in Alabama on March 17, 1944. His father James Wright abandoned the family when Tom was young and went on to

Opposite: The view from St Mary's Road of Ealing Technical College & School of Art, circa the early Sixties. Left: Pete Townshend, the hipster art student.

be a renowned audio engineer in the movie business. Tom's mother Janice remarried Keith Laumer, an officer in the US Air Force, as well as a prolific writer of science fiction in his spare time.

ANTOINETTE SALES [née LAUMER, Tom's half-sister]: Our family often listened to the radio so Tom was exposed to lots of different music at a young age. Because of Dad's job, we moved around, and when in 1956 he got posted to Rangoon, Burma, Tom stayed behind in the States with his uncle and aunt in Birmingham. The uncle was a builder, and Tom worked for him with a predominantly black crew who were probably responsible for instilling in him a love and knowledge of the black blues music of the south. I recall when Tom came out to visit us when he was 13, how excited he was that he had sat next to Fats Domino on part of the trip.

In 1960, when Keith re-enlisted in the US Air Force and was made a captain, the family moved to England, living in a large house at Highfield Place, Mount Pleasant Road in Ealing. While attending the American school on the USAF base in South Ruislip, Tom met Campbell 'Cam' Bruce, from Tulsa, Oklahoma, and, through a mutual associate, his first English friend Tim Bartlett, who hailed from Ealing. Having done menial work after leaving school, Tim was accepted at Ealing Tech, to study graphics. When Tom and Cam graduated, liking what they heard and saw of Tim's life on campus, they successfully enrolled in the photography class at the college.

PETE TOWNSHEND: The photography school was on a different floor and it was quite remote. The art students didn't integrate with the [photography] students very much; they didn't attend our lectures and we didn't hang out with them.

In 1963, when Tom's stepfather got stationed back to America, Tom opted to remain behind. Tim was renting a one-bedroom flat on the top floor of 35 Sunnyside Road, just a stone's throw from the art college, and Tom – soon followed by Cam – moved in. "The flat at Sunnyside," Wright wrote in his memoir *Roadwork*. "That's where I first turned Pete on to pot and American blues."

PETE TOWNSHEND: I was still a virgin – sexually and in many other ways as well. I was living at home with my parents in Woodgrange Avenue, which is just a short walk across Ealing Common to Ealing Tech. Tom and Cam were living nearby on Sunnyside Road, and, appearing exotic creatures through being American, they were really popular with girls, particularly Cam, who was good-looking, slightly effeminate but very beautiful. Tom was quite rugged, more like a redneck kind of guy. He was always pumped up, he did weight lifting, he kept his hair short. Both Tom and Cam liked me and liked what I did, but Tom was the one that sort of adopted me and took me under his wing.

With America still regarded by Brits as the promised land after austerity cast a considerable pall over postwar England, Pete was

Above: Richard 'Barney' Barnes, Pete's close friend whom he met at art college, and the man who came up with the name 'the Who'.

Right: Art school buddies in profile. From left to right: Campbell 'Cam' Bruce, Tom Wright and Tim Bartlett. The photo was taken by Tim Bartlett on his Rayflex camera using a delayed action.

Opposite: A smiling Tom and his girlfriend, Sandy Dawn Glover, at Ealing Tech.

fascinated and intrigued by his new companions, particularly their musical tastes.

PETE TOWNSHEND: I spent quite a bit of time with Tom, just one to one, listening to this great big record collection which was leaned against the wall at Sunnyside Road. They were all American issues, so he'd obviously brought them over. It was like a treasure trove of R&B and it was a bit of an education for me. My dad was a musician and a lot of the members of his band were young so I'd heard a lot of jazz. I'd heard country blues already in Big Bill Broonzy, Lead Belly, and Sonny Terry & Brownie McGhee, so I suppose I'd heard some R&B as well.

Tom's big crushes were Jimmy Reed, Jimmy Smith and Ray Charles. Those were the three who he mainly listened to, and he used to get very stoned. He had a dealer who was associated with Bert Jansch who came down from Glasgow with very high-quality marijuana. Tom was like an advert for what happens when you get stoned and listen to great music; he used to kind of go to this amazing place. I didn't smoke grass with Tom to begin with, but later – I think the following year – I took it for the first time with a girlfriend and wasn't particularly crazy about it.

According to Richard Barnes, who also became a friend of Tom's, the Sunnyside Road collection consisted of over 100 records, which Barnes details in *Maximum R&B* as including "all of Jimmy Reed's albums, all of Chuck Berry's, all of James Brown's, Bo Diddley, John Lee Hooker, Snooks Eaglin, Mose Allison, all of Jimmy Smith's, Muddy Waters, Lightnin' Hopkins, Howlin' Wolf, Slim Harpo, Buddy Guy, Big Bill Broonzy, Sonny Terry & Brownie McGhee, Joe Turner, Nina Simone, Booker T & The M.G.'s, Little Richard, Jerry Lee Lewis, Carl Perkins, the Isley Brothers, Fats Domino, the Coasters, Ray Charles, Jimmy McGriff, Brother Jack McDuff, John Patton, Bobby Bland, the Drifters, the Shirelles, the Impressions, and many jazz albums including Charlie Parker, Charles Mingus, John Coltrane, Miles Davis, Milt Jackson, Wes Montgomery, Jimmy Giuffre, Dave Brubeck, plus albums by Jonathan Winters, Mort Sahl, Shelley Berman and particularly Lord Buckley. There were also about 30 classical albums."

Townshend recalls there not being "any early Tamla-Motown at all, and Booker T & The M.G.'s was about the only Memphis stuff that Tom had. Bob Dylan came along a bit later so he didn't have any Dylan – I'm sure he would have done. Tom and Cam's tastes were communal, but I think Cam's was slightly softer. Both really liked Julie London, which I couldn't get."

TIM BARTLETT: Tom and Cam tend to get the credit for having all these great records, but I have to say, some of them were actually mine. I bought an awful lot of albums from Collet's in Charing Cross Road, which was a great source of rare imports. I got into Big Bill Broonzy and John Lee Hooker and those sorts of people, so I'd say about 25 per cent were mine. Tom also brought an original Fender Stratocaster guitar back from America, and we all tried to play along with these sounds.

Tom's youthful chutzpah extended to persuading the owner of the Allday Café (aka Sid's Café) – a greasy spoon popular with the art

Above: Cam (left), unknown, and Tom on the stairs near the main entrance to Ealing Tech. Right: Cam and the hash pipe he brought back from Morocco.

Right: Original UK copy of Booker T and The M.G.s' 'Green Onions' 45, 1962. Membership card for the Ealing Club.

students, situated around the corner from the college at 94 Warwick Road – into letting him put records on the jukebox.

PETE TOWNSHEND: The song that I remember sounding really, really great was Booker T's 'Green Onions'. There were a few others that stood out, like Mose Allison's 'Parchman Farm', but 'Green Onions' was the one. Sid's Café was a hangout where we mixed with the fashion students who were mostly pretty girls, one of whom I later married.

At the same time, a new musical revolution uncannily ignited just yards from Sunnyside Road and the art college. In March 1962, British rhythm and blues pioneers Alexis Korner and Cyril Davies had started a regular Saturday night club date for like-minded blues enthusiasts at the Ealing Club, situated below the ABC tea shop, opposite Ealing Broadway station. It was in this basement venue that members of the fledgling Rolling Stones, Animals, Manfred Mann and Cream first performed or sat in as part of Korner's band, Blues Incorporated. As its popularity snowballed, R&B moved in from the suburbs, replacing trad jazz as the hip music of choice in London's clubland throughout 1963.

PETE TOWNSHEND: I remember setting eyes on the Stones for the first time. They were coming out of Ealing Broadway station, the whole band as it was then – without [piano player] Ian Stewart who had been sacked. They were obviously heading over to the club. They were just so magnetic.

With the emergence of the Beatles and the Rolling Stones, and the Sixties' febrile arts scene as typified at Ealing, it seemed the possibilities were endless in a London that was just starting to swing. Unfortunately, for Tom and Cam, it was the end of the road. Acting on a tip-off, police raided the flat at Sunnyside Road and the pair were busted for possession of pot (fortuitously, Tim was away at his parents' in Norfolk). After a custodial period in the Young Offenders Institution in Feltham, they were given the choice of a prison sentence or immediately vacating the country.

PETE TOWNSHEND: Mareka, Cam's girlfriend, and another girl inherited the flat. Barney and I were living on the floor below, and the records were left behind in our care. We became the replacements for Tom and Cam for a while. We didn't just inherit

the record collection, we inherited the girls, and, to a lesser extent, the drugs. When Tom and Cam were ordered to leave, I recall they rapidly tried to record all the albums, over about five days, and because they were in such a hurry, they left the tapes behind. I occasionally listened to those tapes and I found some very interesting things on there that I'd not heard before, so I don't know whether some of the albums went sideways or whether Tom and Cam tried to take some with them, but the tapes were a comprehensive record of the entire collection.

While the teenage art student and musician continued to soak up these exotic influences, Tom and Cam left England under a cloud at the end of 1963. The drug bust had frightened and shaken them up. Cam went home to America, but Tom headed for Paris and then to the Balearics, where he drifted around for a couple of years while continuing his interest in photography.

PETE TOWNSHEND: Barney tells a story that I ended up with the records, but I sent them all back to Tom while he was in Formentera. Barney and I had tried to do it ourselves a couple of times. Also, Mareka took about a third of the albums that she said Cam wanted. I made a meticulous list of everything, and by the time I was up at my new flat in Chesham Place, Belgravia [in mid-1965], I'd replaced every single record, and I've still got them all.

In the summer of 1964, Pete approached his final days as an art student on the eve of becoming a professional musician with the Who.

PETE TOWNSHEND: Even though the band were gigging fairly heavily, I would still go to college when I could until the time when my course leader, Robin Ray, asked me how much I was earning. I told him '20 quid a week.' He said, 'Pete, that's more than what I'm getting!' There were a couple of guys in our graphics course who were about 26. They were ex-army because they'd had to do National Service. In those days, they were allowed to come back to higher education when they got out of the forces and start again. So Robin said, 'Anytime you want to come back, you can come back.' I left and at the end of that year 'I Can't Explain' was a hit for the Who, and I was away.

Tom Wright and Pete Townshend only knew each other at art college for roughly a year, but their meeting and friendship would play a significant part in their subsequent career paths.

TIM BARTLETT: It's true to say that Tom made his mark while at Ealing. He had an extraordinary ability to draw people to him, and he was certainly one of the most charismatic people I've ever met. But England made something of Tom that he wouldn't have had if he'd stayed in America. I can't think he would have been the same guy. The Ealing experience enriched his life immeasurably.

Left: Pete in Sid's Café, the local Ealing Tech hangout, with fellow students. From left to right: Dave Duce, Mareka and unknown.

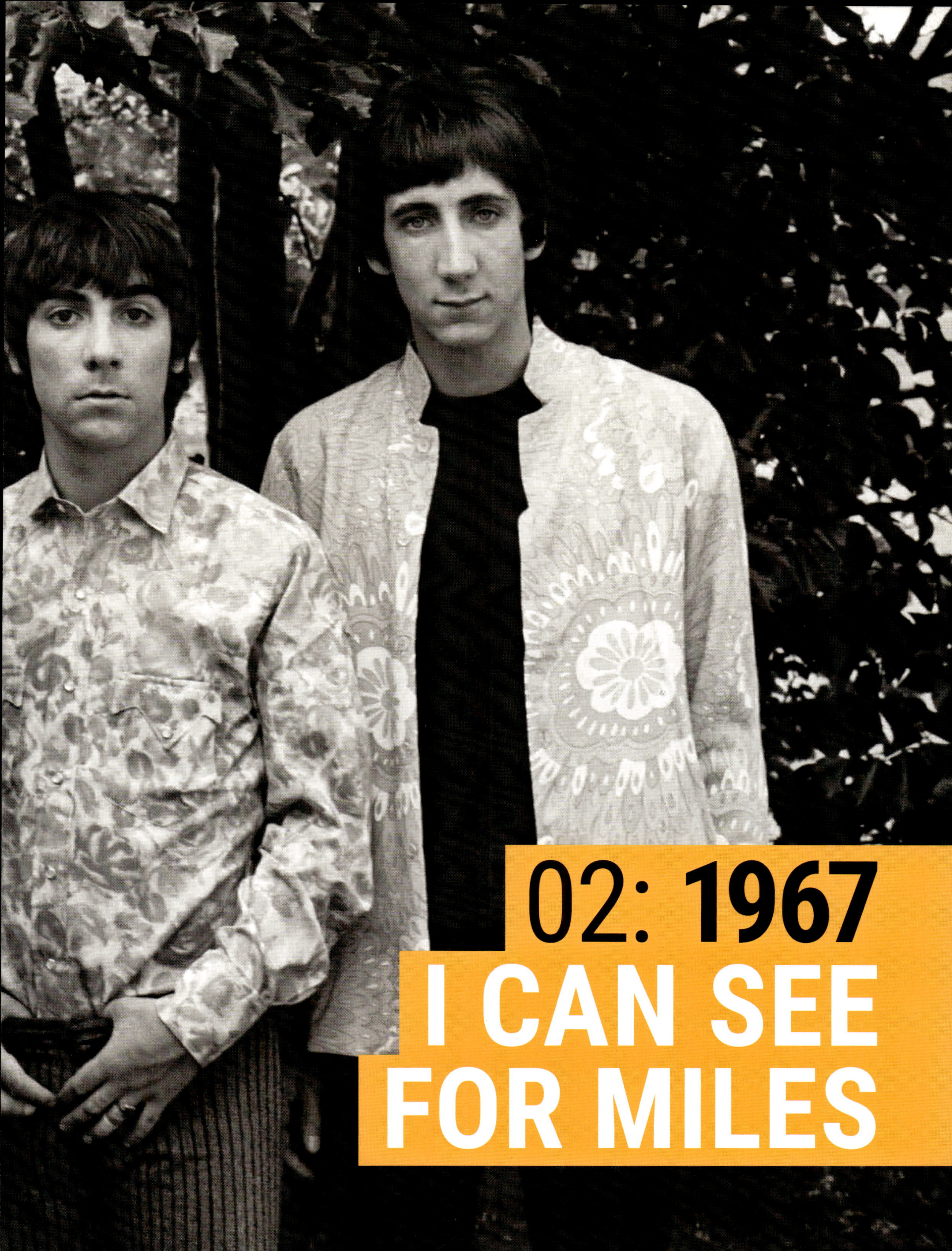

02: 1967
I CAN SEE FOR MILES

Left: Tour programme for Herman's Hermits' 1967 US tour featuring the Who.

Above: Early publicity for the Who in America.

Opposite left: Programme for the Murray the K season, Easter 1967, New York, featuring the Who.

Right: A pensive-looking Tom on the DC7 used to fly the Herman's Hermits tour around America.

By 1967, the Who had risen to become one of the top groups in Britain, thanks to six consecutive hit singles ('I Can't Explain', 'Anyway Anyhow Anywhere', 'My Generation', 'Substitute', 'I'm A Boy', 'Happy Jack') and a stage act notorious for both its loudness and its brash 'auto-destructive' finale. The latter was inspired by the eradicative demonstrations given by German performance artist Gustav Metzger that Pete had witnessed at Ealing Art College. "We'd get paid 500 quid for a concert," John Entwistle recalled, "but Pete would smash up a £250 guitar, and with expenses at £150, you didn't get that much afterwards. We all lived as though we were making 300 quid a week and we were making 20. The first time we came to the States we weren't earning much, but we had great clothes and good equipment."

The Who's managers, Kit Lambert and Chris Stamp, had found it difficult to launch the band over the Atlantic, despite the American music industry having been in thrall to 'the British Invasion' over the past few years. The Who's quirky and eccentric Englishness was not as easily marketable as the Beatles' universality or the sensual rebelliousness of the Rolling Stones, and light years removed from the clean-cut wholesomeness of the Dave Clark Five and Herman's Hermits. The problem was compounded by the Who being signed to a conservative record label, Decca, who were fairly clueless as to how to market such a modern and unconventional group. Because of this, the Who's British hits had been unceremonious flops in North America (although 'My Generation' reached number three in Canada), but they had gained a zealous following among Anglophile kids, particularly in New York, Detroit, Chicago and Los Angeles, and in the repertoires of various American garage groups.

The Who had to be *seen* for their full effect. An initially mooted Stateside foray for the band in September 1966 was cancelled, reportedly due to visa troubles. Stamp went looking for an American booking agency to place the Who with and ended up at Premier Talent in New York.

Having worked for the mighty General Artists Corporation, Frank Barsalona left to set up his own company, Premier Talent Associates, in 1964. While record companies in the Fifties and Sixties rarely backed tours for performers without a hit record to promote, Barsalona established a different business model – an independent concert system autonomous from the main record companies – by creating a network of young, attuned promoters around America such as Bill Graham in San Francisco, Ron Delsener in New York and Don Law in Boston, who could raise the capital necessary to back rock acts' tours – both known and unknown.

Over Easter week of 1967, the Who and Cream made their American concert debuts in a season at the RKO 58th St. Theatre, New York, dubbed 'Murray the K's Music in the Fifth Dimension'. Since the late Fifties, popular DJ Murray Kaufman had promoted rock shows at the Brooklyn Fox, featuring multi-artist bills playing up to five performances per day, catering to kids on school vacation. These usually started in the morning, lasting right into the evening. In January 1967, Beatles manager Brian Epstein's NEMS Enterprises amalgamated with the Robert Stigwood Organisation agency (which represented the Who and Cream). Undoubtedly, the Epstein connection helped persuade Kaufman – the self-dubbed 'Fifth Beatle' – to add both of these unknown British bands to an already-crammed bill.

According to a contemporary report in *Hit Parader*: "Generally, the 10-day Murray the K show in New York was disappointing. Although it featured Mitch Ryder, Wilson Pickett, the Blues Project, Jim & Jean, the Mandala, the Hardly-Worthit Players, the Chicago Loop, the Who and the Cream and one-night-only guest stars Simon & Garfunkel, the Blues Magoos and Phil Ochs, with the Rascals, and the Vagrants added in a desperate last-minute attempt to save the show, audience reaction was apathetic.

"Except for the guest stars, none of the acts had more than 10 minutes on stage. Some did only one or two songs. The films being projected while artists were performing were distracting. It was a bad scene… The Who had to pay for the 12 microphones they broke during [the run]. They had a really wild act. Pete Townshend broke three guitars."

PETE TOWNSHEND: We did this very short set where we played only two songs, and at the end of which we smashed our gear, so I spent a lot of my time repairing guitars.

Despite not receiving any major television exposure, 'Happy Jack' rose up the American charts and eventually reached number 24 on *Billboard*, and as high as 13 on *Cash Box* in early June '67. Its success paved the way for the Who's return to play the important three-day Monterey International Pop Festival in California, preceded by small warm-up shows in Detroit, Chicago and Bill Graham's Fillmore Auditorium in San Francisco. The Who's incendiary performance on the final evening at Monterey stunned the blissed-out crowd – and word started to spread.

PETE TOWNSHEND: In the years after Tom left England, I'd occasionally get messages from him. He would send me photographs from the Balearics and they were very strange. I couldn't quite get his arty style. He also sent a few musical tips, some of which jibed with me, some of which didn't, and I could see that he was still serious about his music.

Tom's carefree, footloose time in Europe came to an abrupt end when he was badly beaten up in Ibiza. He returned home to his family in San Antonio.

ANTOINETTE SALES [Tom's half-sister]: After Texas, the family moved to Florida where my father bought 'the Island', which was a peninsula in a lake about an hour north of Tampa. Tom became the photographer at Weeki Wachee Springs State Park, a tourist attraction two miles up the highway. It was a deep natural spring that featured a sunken small amphitheatre fitted with lights and a glass wall where the audience sat to watch 'mermaids' swimming around… Being surrounded by bathing beauties, Tom was in his element.

In 1967, Antoinette heard on the radio that the Who were coming to play in Florida, with teenybop headliners Herman's Hermits. She pressed her brother to get in touch and reconnect with his old friend.

ANTOINETTE SALES: Tom was reluctant to bother Pete so my best friend and I picked up the local phone book and started calling every hotel in the area until we found where the Who were staying and left a message for Pete: 'Call Tom Wright at this number. I'm here in Tampa.' Pete called back quickly. He told Tom he had been searching everywhere for him.

Tom and his sister were invited to the show that evening (July 31, 1967) at the Bayfront Center Arena in St. Petersburg. As Tom wrote in his memoir *Roadwork*: "I remember feeling very sorry for Herman's Hermits… I was sure that after the Who's set everyone would have to leave, things had gone so badly – Pete banging his guitar, splinters flying everywhere. The music was so loud it had felt like we were standing inside a jet engine. Surely it was the end of Pete, the end of concerts in Florida, I'd thought. A deejay at the side of the stage, his eyes wide, ears ringing, could only mumble, 'Wow, wow, wow,' over and over. The audience didn't know if they liked it or not. They'd come to see Herman, but they'd gotten bulldozed in the face by the Who."

Afterwards Tom and Antoinette went out for dinner with the Who, where the erstwhile Ealing art students had a chance to properly reconnect. Pete told Tom that the Who needed updated publicity photos to send back to England, and invited him to accompany the band on the road. Tom made an on-the-spot decision to quit his job and leave the next day to go on tour. As he summated, "The Who came to Florida, and that was the end of the underwater photography career."

Mississippi State Coliseum, Jackson, MI, August 1, 1967

The first Who show that Tom documented – just over two weeks into the Who's first nationwide American tour, supporting Herman's Hermits.

Hailing from Manchester, and fronted by gap-toothed pop idol Peter Noone, Herman's Hermits were at the peak of their abnormal popularity in America, having ranked top singles act ahead of the Beatles in 1965 (according to *Billboard*), and with 11 Top 10 hits to their credit. Both the Who and Herman's Hermits were with the same booking agency, Premier Talent, so to get the Who exposure, it didn't seem unusual by the standards of the day to pair both groups together, despite their wildly varying styles. (A similar thing happened at exactly the same time when the Jimi Hendrix Experience played their first US tour as support act for the Monkees.)

In a British music magazine *Beat Instrumental* article (dated December '67), Kit Lambert claimed that the Who worked up a rock version of the Nancy Sinatra and Lee Hazlewood hit 'Jackson' specially for this show, but this has never been confirmed by an eyewitness account. What is beyond dispute is the Who waved large Confederate flags at the climax of the stage destruction during the last number 'My Generation' before leaving the stage – perhaps not the wisest of moves from the vantage of these more enlightened times.

The
Who

Outdoor photo session, Jackson, MI, August 2, 1967

Tom's baptism of fire continued with a photo shoot he hastily organised in a rolling field on the outskirts of Jackson. Using a Rolliflex and a Nikon, Tom shot in both black and white and colour, the four band members in individual poses and as a group, with various costume changes including their stage costumes – John's Union Jack and Welsh dragon jackets, Roger's Edwardian lace and ruffles, and Pete's paisley smock. "Standing alone, they all looked fine," Tom recalled. "Side by side, though, it was way out of sync. All those colours clashed, not like the Beatles who all looked so similar in their photos. But maybe that's what they wanted. More than likely they didn't think about it much."

PETE TOWNSHEND: The Monterey kaftan and a ten-gallon hat which doesn't suit me at all. The Who were in such an interesting place in this crossover period. I was processing what was going on, and I was very much looking at changing the way that we operated. My girlfriend Karen was dressing me in these Syd Barrett, psychedelic kind of outfits, and I was getting fed up with the psychedelic image, this kind of girly look.

During the session, Wright let off coloured smoke bombs to heighten the sense of transported Brits in an alien landscape. As he recalled in *Roadwork*: "I lined up the band and set up my tripod in front of them. With my cigarette, I lit as many smoke bombs as I could hold in my right hand and then tossed them, all at once, behind the band. Then I ran back to the camera. I could get two or three shots before the haze, stinking of smouldering garbage and wet firecracker fuses, drifted away.

"When I ran out of smoke bombs and film, we headed for the car. Up the hill, about 200 yards from our rented station wagon, someone was running toward us with a stick – or maybe it was a gun. We couldn't tell. The band dove into the back seats, I spun the car around, and we flew down the dirt road. The rabid farmer quickly disappeared in swirling clouds of dust. We laughed all the way back to town."

Above: A young Keith Moon looking sweet and innocent.

"If we had four days off in one spot with nothing happening," Tom remembered in 1998, "I knew for a fact on the fourth day that I would be talking to either law enforcement or hotel management because you couldn't lock Keith up in a motel room in Nebraska for four days without something explosive happening.

"I would say to Keith, 'Well, it's Saturday night, we got a show tomorrow on Sunday, there's not gonna be any music stores open so don't break all your drum heads and sticks.' 'OK,' he would say. Every time I said something like that, I later learned that I just guaranteed total devastation, not just slight damage but he'd wipe everything out."

PETE TOWNSHEND: A lot of what Keith was doing was to antagonise Tom. He had a chip on his shoulder about Tom, I'm not quite sure why, but the mischief really got out of hand and that was where Keith's antics with cherry bombs really kicked off.

Airport runway, Memphis, TN, August 15, 1967

In the days before luxury travel in private jets, the Herman's Hermits–Who tour covered the long distances via a chartered DC7 plane. Because transport was strictly economy, this could lead to some nerve-shredding moments. En route to Nashville, one of the plane's engines caught fire, necessitating an emergency landing in Memphis on a foam-covered runway. Tom's photos show Pete and Keith seeing the lighter side of what could have been far more serious. "That was a bleedin' nightmare," John Entwistle recalled in 1976, "because two blokes on the plane were out of their heads on acid."

"I never regarded myself as a person afraid of travelling by air," Pete reflected. "When we did the Herman's Hermits tour in an old charter plane, I wrote so many songs about plane crashes, it was incredible." One of these, 'Glow Girl' – a song about a doomed couple's reincarnation after an air crash – was recorded in 1968 but not released until the Who's *Odds & Sods* collection in 1974.

209

Opposite (top): Roger in reflective mood.

Opposite (bottom): Pete backstage at the Memorial Auditorium, Chattanooga, TN with manager and mentor, Kit Lambert, August 17, 1967.

PETE TOWNSHEND: Kit was dropping into the tour at various points, flying in and out, while we travelled by bus!

Left: Pete with a distinctive Gibson SG double-neck EDS-1275 6/12-string guitar that he'd bought on tour.

PETE TOWNSHEND: I don't know where that guitar came from, but it broke on my hip. I was banging it on my hip and it split in two so I carved a bit out of it and put it back together at an angle so the necks were off kilter. It played fine though.

Bradley's Barn, Nashville, TN, August 17, 1967

The Who's early recording career was scattershot by nature, with sessions crammed into a frantic schedule of gigs, radio, TV and photo sessions. Because their managers, Kit Lambert and Chris Stamp, wanted the Who's third album released by the end of 1967, recording sessions were booked in New York, Nashville and Los Angeles during breaks in the Hermits tour. Lambert brought the master tapes of unfinished tracks over from London for overdubs to be applied. Bradley's Barn, a former cattle barn situated 20 miles from downtown Nashville, was set up in 1964 by Owen Bradley, the vice president of Decca Records' Nashville division, and numerous country and pop artists such as Brenda Lee and Roy Orbison recorded there. (The building burned down in 1980.)

In these photos, Pete and John add vocal harmonies and overdubs to several tracks.

PETE TOWNSHEND: Bradley's Barn was full of spiders! It was quite strange working in there; the equipment was old-fashioned – a control room with four knobs. John and I would have done some backing vocal work on 'I Can See For Miles' here. At the end of this trip, we went into the famous studio Gold Star in LA, where Phil Spector recorded, and that's where we mastered it.

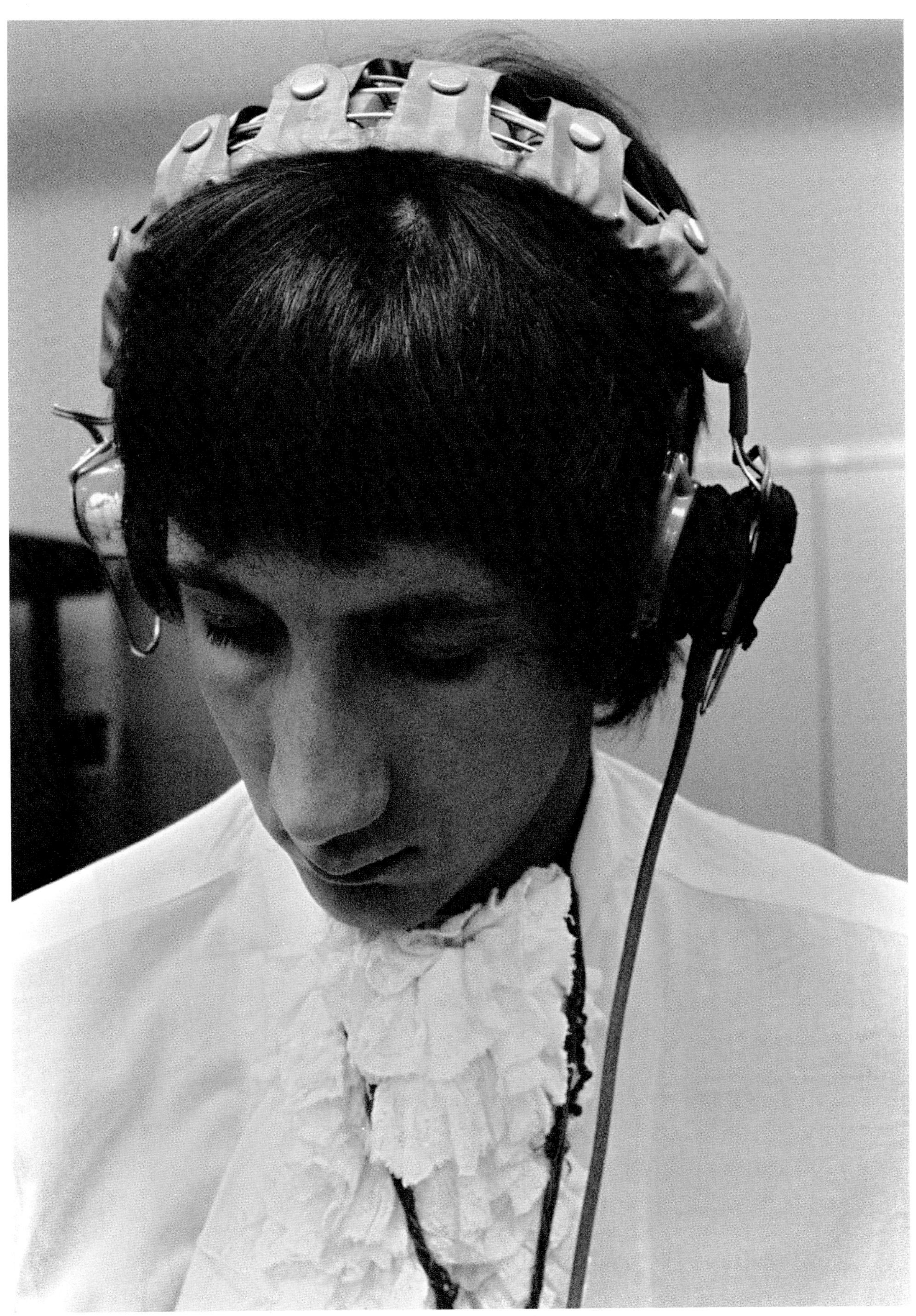

Life on the road, captured by Tom's lens.

Right: Standing behind John Entwistle is Ron Gilbert, bass player of fellow tour support act the Blues Magoos, from New York, who had scored a US Top 5 hit earlier that year with '(We Ain't Got) Nothin' Yet'.

PETE TOWNSHEND: I was very friendly with the Blues Magoos and got indoctrinated with them into the idea that the world might be invaded by creatures from outer space. This was just post the big LSD trip I'd taken on the flight home from the Monterey festival, which was life-changing for me.

We would have been on the bus to the plane or to the gig. What was interesting to me about America at the time was that it all looked the same. What was different occasionally was coming across proper rednecks who carried guns, particularly policemen, and they hated the fact that we had long hair. They'd read the hippie stories that were coming out of California and it felt to me like real prejudice. They were very old-fashioned from our point of view. Apart from that, it just looked all the fucking same.

TRANSFER ISSUED AS FARE PAID
PLEASE
Do not carry
on unnecessary
conversation
with operator
while bus is
in motion

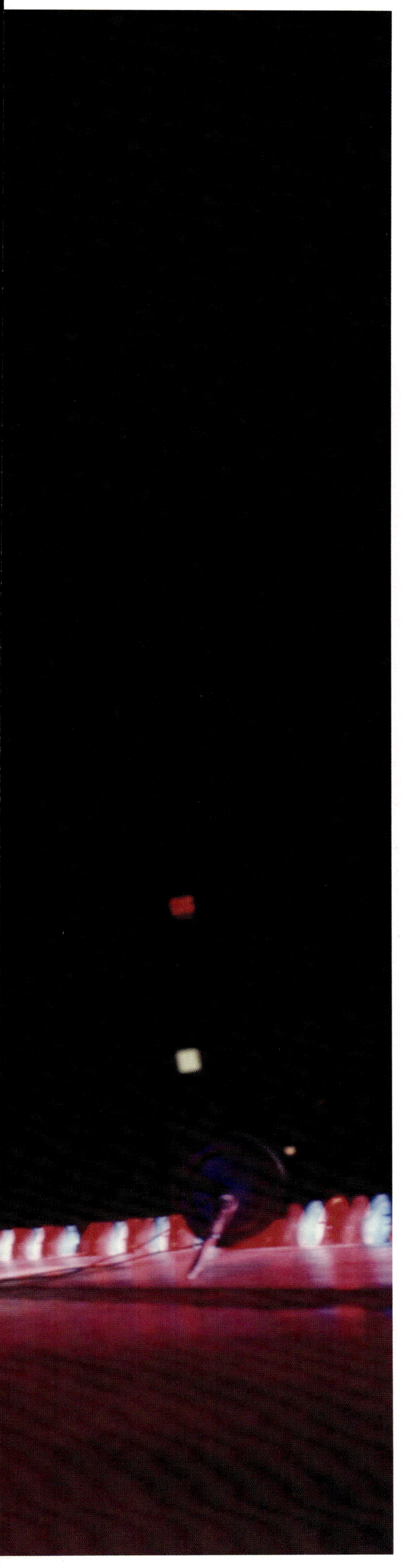

Minneapolis Auditorium, Minneapolis, MN, August 20, 1967

PETE TOWNSHEND: In a sense, we were trying to find our feet, and this tour was 10 weeks of feeling lost really; playing for only half an hour. I remember we used to play things like 'Substitute', 'I'm A Boy', 'Happy Jack' and finish with 'My Generation'. It was all over very, very quickly. We'd do our act, smash our gear and then onto the next town.

Pete on motel balcony, Edmonton, Canada, August 21, 1967

PETE TOWNSHEND: We stayed in Holiday Inns, which were meant to be a home from home so they were all identical for people who lived on the road. I got very fond of them; lots of my early song lyrics are written on Holiday Inn stationery. I carried a studio with me. I had a Nagra and another Wollensak tape machine and I made a few demos on the road.

Tom learned to use his temporary surroundings as a makeshift darkroom; as events unfolded on tour, reams of film were processed and printed in numerous motel bathrooms.

PETE TOWNSHEND: What was interesting about Edmonton was that there were Mods, and we were post-Mod. But they were still very much into being Mods – they were kids from a whole community from somewhere in London who had moved to Canada, and they took the fashion they had and they'd sustained it. So they were looking forward to seeing us and we show up and we're a bunch of hippies wearing psychedelic clothes.

HAPPY BIRTHDAY KEITH
Flint, MI, August 23, 1967

PETE TOWNSHEND: It went to his head. *Sgt. Pepper* was out and Keith believed he was Mr. Kite [from the album's song 'Being For The Benefit Of Mr. Kite!'].

Because Detroit was experiencing severe upheaval due to race riots and civil unrest, the Hermits tour played some 60 miles north of the city, in Flint. That day was Keith's 21st birthday – an event that has assumed fantastical proportions in Who folklore. As evidenced by the photo opposite, the Holiday Inn was initially welcoming to the guest of honour, but their hospitality would be severely tested following the evening's sparsely attended show at Atwood Stadium.

Right (top): Keith with tour publicist and Kit Lambert and Chris Stamp's assistant Nancy Lewis, who was later instrumental in breaking Monty Python into America. Nancy, who organised Keith's birthday party, arranged for Premier and Decca to present him with a five-tiered drum-shaped cake.

PETE TOWNSHEND: Nancy was from Detroit and had worked at Motown, so she'd been in the studio and she told us great stories about how they did stuff. Whenever I meet any of the Tamla people who are still going, they remember her very fondly.

Right (bottom): Pete and Keith in conference backstage with loyal road manager Bob Pridden. Bob started with the Who in December 1966 and graduated to become their sound technician in 1969 – a position he held until his retirement in 2016.

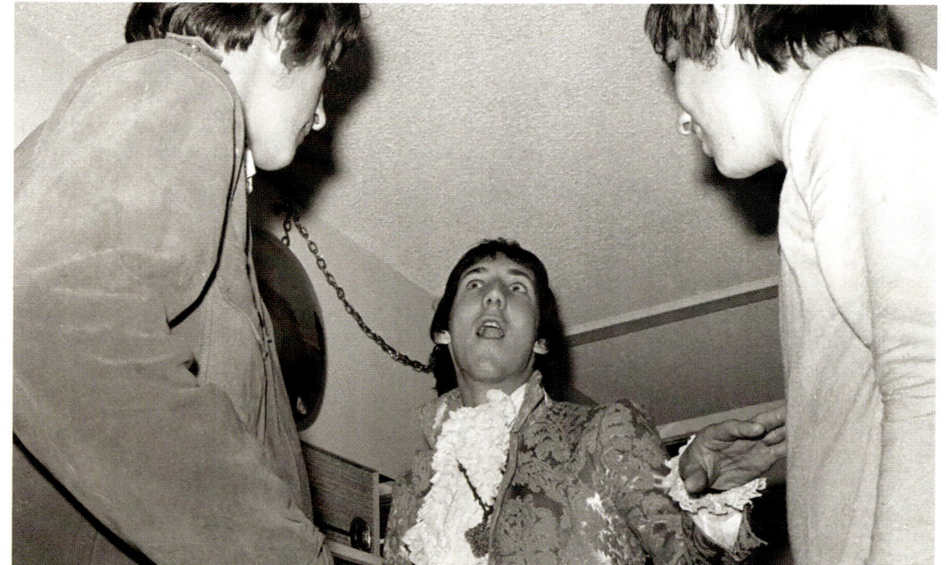

Holiday Inn
OF AMERICA
HAPPY
BIRTHDAY
KEITH

Above: The calm before the storm. John, Keith and Roger with Kit Lambert (centre) outside the Flint Holiday Inn.

After the concert, the birthday bash escalated into a rowdy shindig. Responding to noise complaints, the hotel manager informed the partygoers there was a midnight curfew. "I knew that wasn't going to sit well with anybody," Tom told Richard Barnes. "I told him we'd wind it down and he left. At one minute after 12, he comes running back and says, 'Goddammit, this sounds more like a revolution than a birthday party...' He was just about to go into a big deal when Keith picked up what was left of the five-tiered cake and just shoved it into this guy's face. Everybody in the room went silent, including this guy."

The police were summoned and Moon ended up with a broken front tooth, supposedly while trying to beat a hasty retreat from the scene. While Tom's images document the start of the party, it would appear he left his cameras behind, as his considerable archive doesn't contain a single image of the mayhem; a pity, because if a Lincoln Continental actually *did* end up in the Holiday Inn's swimming pool as rock'n'roll legend has it, Tom's lens would have no doubt captured the act.

PETE TOWNSHEND: Funnily enough, I don't remember being a part of it, although I think they had a lot of fun. I don't have any other memory other than Keith having an altercation with some fan. I was there watching it and the kid's father came up with the son and said, 'What the fuck's going on here?' I said, 'It's his 21st birthday, he's out of it', and the guy went off. I sort of hustled Keith away. Then the police arrived and they were looking for Keith and he hid in my bedroom. Other than that, I don't know.

MARCH OF
DIMES

Atwood Stadium, Flint, MI, August 23, 1967

PETE TOWNSHEND: Of course, by now Jimi Hendrix had taken over the scene, both in London's clubs and also at Monterey Pop. Funnily enough, when we played in Washington, DC [on August 13], I met up with Cam [from art school] because that's where he went to live, and we went together to see Jimi and Jimi played '...Can't Explain'. He knew we were there. I introduced Cam to him afterwards. Jimi was never really that friendly to me until the very end. One day we were in LA, I went to see him and he was a little bit drunk and a little bit stoned but he was really sweet to me, and he died soon after.

MARCH OF
DIMES

A KISS

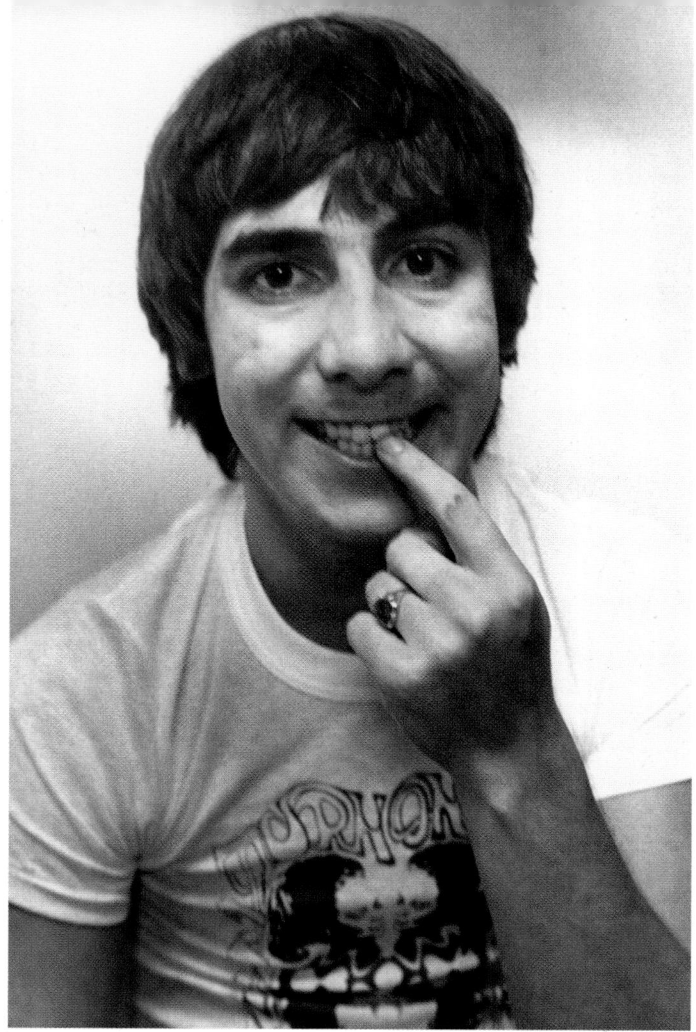

PETE TOWNSHEND: Roger talks about not being a drinker like the rest of us. I think he would have liked leapers but he didn't take them because they fucked up his voice, so he said. His addiction was women. If he couldn't get a woman, he would get angry and bitter and irritated, but if he was with a girl, he was fabulous. In New York, for the Murray the K shows, his girlfriend [later wife] Heather fixed him up with a friend of hers and Roger was just a delight right the way through.

Left: Keith pointing to his new front tooth, the work of a Michigan dentist after the drummer's birthday pratfall. Because he was so drunk, Moon had to be operated on without anaesthetic.

Below: The Who give an interview for a local TV station. The tour attracted media attention in most cities on the itinerary. As Tom remembered: "The biggest question that people had for the Who in those days was 'Do you guys know the Beatles?'"

Flying to St. Louis, MI, August 25, 1967

Left: Keith, with portable record player on his lap, talking to Karl Green, the bass player of Herman's Hermits.

PETE TOWNSHEND: We liked Karl – he was a bit of a raver. This [tour] was the end of the road for Herman's Hermits in America. I remember my first trip to New York [in June 1966], going to meet Allen Klein, and I was on the same plane as them. When we landed, there were all these little Herman fans and a couple of them came up and attached themselves to me, and they're still Who fans to this day.

Overleaf: The Who playing at Kiel Opera House, borrowing the Hermits' Fender Showman amps and cabinets. Small wonder members of Herman's Hermits are anxiously looking on from the wings.

PETE TOWNSHEND: I obviously wasn't smashing guitars every night. It was mainly showmanship. If I smashed one, it was serious stuff. It was definitely art!

For the tour, John used a Sunn amp and cabinets, while Pete used Thomas Organ US Vox Super Beatle amps. Keith had brought over his new customised Premier drum kit, which comprised three mounted toms, three 16-inch floor toms, a semi-locked hi-hat, three cymbals and a pair of 22-inch bass drums. These were emblazoned with 'Pictures of Lily' Victorian nudes, the Who 3D logo and the legend 'Keith Moon – Patent British Exploding Drummer'.

Above and opposite: John and Keith on a riverboat somewhere in America. Among all the internal tension created by the Who's differing personalities, Entwistle and Moon had the closest alliance. Their pranks on tour included keeping a piranha fish in a hotel bath and buying a lobster on ice at an airport, whose claw acted as their room key holder.

PETE TOWNSHEND: In the early Who days, it became clear to me that John and Keith had set up a kind of friendship where Roger and I were outsiders. And so, although Roger and I didn't align, we didn't create an alternative partnership – we couldn't have done, we were so different.

PETE TOWNSHEND: It's funny seeing John looking so young. This shows the hanging around. We used to get incredibly bored.

As well as providing vocal back-up, John also got the chance to sing lead on his composition 'Boris The Spider' [from 1966's *A Quick One*] during the Who's set.

Outdoor photo session, Ohio, early September 1967

PETE TOWNSHEND: These are great photos; they make us look good and they're well composed.

Civic Arena, Pittsburgh, PA, September 3, 1967

The summer Herman's Hermits trek, which began on July 13 in Calgary, Canada, closed on September 9 in Honolulu, a nine-week coast-to-coast jaunt on which the package often played two – occasionally three – shows in one day. The tour was a gruelling experience, to put it mildly. "It got us around America," said Roger, "but it did us no good at all."

"I had to borrow $100 to get home first class to make it look good," John recalled. "Truthfully, we didn't make a cent from our first US tour. We were always in debt."

Premier
THE WHO

Premier
THE WHO
Premier
THE WHO

Union Catholic High School, Scotch Plains, NJ, November 29, 1967

When the Who arrived back in England, they had a brief period of rest before throwing themselves into a further round of one-nighters around Britain, as well as an 11-date theatre tour headlining over Traffic, the Herd and the Tremeloes. On top of this they completed recording their third album *The Who Sell Out*, released in time for Christmas.

With their latest single 'I Can See For Miles' on the *Billboard* chart at number 11 (it reached its highest peak at 9 two weeks later), the Who returned to America on November 15 for a brief two-week whistle-stop tour taking in the Midwest, California and the Eastern seaboard, either headlining or as a support act. Tom's vast photographic archive inexplicably has few images from this tour; all that could be accessed were shots from this gig in a New Jersey school gymnasium.

When the Who returned to England, Pete confidently told the *NME*: "I honestly feel that in America we have reached the same measure of success it's taken us three years to attain in Europe. The group has been getting a great feeling of satisfaction from the dates we've played. We'd like to reach the stage where our record success becomes secondary to concerts, and I think we might be getting there."

NIGHT OF STARS

SPECTACULAR

Next Fri., March 22

the World's Most Sensational group. Taking America by STORM.

CURTIS HIXON

THE **WHO**

Direct from England the only group that Destroys their Equipment when done playing.

5 BANDS

LOST ELEMENT, ROLLINS 5 & OTHERS

$4.50, $3.50, $3.00 & $2.50

TICKETS ON SALE BOX OFFICE

Tampa: Sears, Belk-Lindsey

St. Pete: Sears

THE WHO

IN CONCERT

Plus

THE DECOYS

Wednesday, Nov. 29, 1967 - 8:00 p. m.

UNION CATHOLIC HIGH SCHOOL

1600 MARTINE AVE. SCOTCH PLAINS, N. J.

Donation $2.50

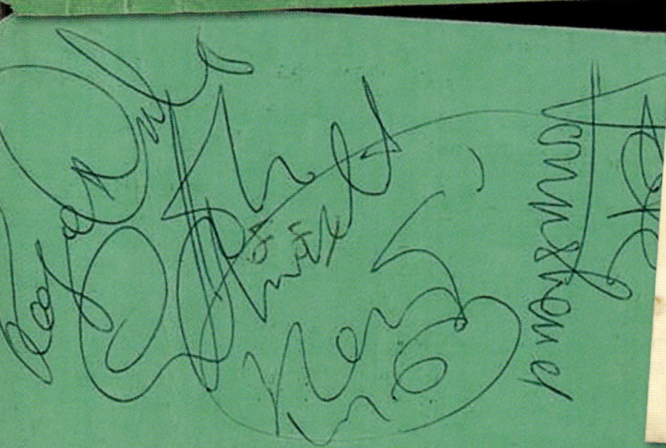

"MY GENERATION"

"I CAN SEE FOR

The WH

AT EXPOSITION GARDENS

MARCH 10

3 P.M. till 6 P.M

Tickets On Sale At...

PEORIA MUSICAL

HI FI ONE STOP

SHERIDAN VILLAGE RECORD SHOP

DON'T BE BORED ON SUNDAY — COME TO THE SHO

THE ROUND SOUNDS GO ON AND ON AND ON AND ON AN

THE WHO

WESTBURY MUSIC FAIR

ONE NIGHT ONLY MAR. 30-8:30 P.M.

PRICES: $4.50, 3.50, 2.50. RES: Call (516) 333-0533.

Mail Orders Write: Westbury Music Fair, Box 86, Westbury, Long Island, N.Y. 11590

Enclose stamped, self-addressed envelope.

IN CONCERT

OP SCENE

How in The Who do they draw crowds?

"They" are the brains behind all those broken instruments

By JAY DURWOOD

a recent report, Iain bin, manager of the Queen abeth theatre complex, ted out that some rock ds were just not welcome he theatre.

's not the music that cons the Queen Elizabeth agement, but the audi-. Any band which has a itation of causing a disance through provocation heer popularity is told to elsewhere for a place to form.

Elsewhere is usually the Agrodome, where seats are less vulnerable. This time the group is The Who. This British rock group lead in their chosen field of disruption, if their custom of breaking up their instruments on stage is any guide.

Other groups, American and British, have picked up the custom, and The Who, according to advance reports, have stopped breaking up instruments in England.

But according to The Who's staff of publicity men, the guitar-braking will continue on their North American tour, including Vancouver tonight at 8 p.m. in the Agrodome.

There are those who may well suspect that The Who's music is written by these same publicity men, or at least some exceptional imitations.

For instance, their LP entitled "The Who Sell Out." Instead of just music, the album is a spoof of the standard Top 40 radio station, or in the case of their country, pirate radio.

Between songs are spoof commercials of such products as Heinz baked beans and deodorants, as well as some real, but now extinct, spot jingles from the English pirate stations.

With Peter Townsend, Roger Daltrey, Keith Moon and John Entwhisltle, the resultant show at the Agrodome should have a little more shock and comedy than the standard rock performance.

Next Friday at the PNE, another rock group with a more soulful sound appears at 9 p.m. in the Gardens Auditorium. Paul Butterfield and his Blues Band, accompanied by the Retina Circus light show, will demonstrate how to bridge the gap between blues and rock with a Chicago sound.

Paul Butterfield plays a harmonica cupped close to any handy microphone to produce a unique electric instrument.

42 days of Who destruction

The Who, currently touring Australia and New Zealand, may also tour Japan before beginning a Stateside jaunt on February 20.

This time their U. S. tour will last six weeks and will give the British group the largest opportunity yet to reach their vast number of fans. Beginning at the Fillmore in San Francisco February 21-25, they are expected to tour their way east to New York, but negotiations for dates are still going on.

Famed for smashing their expensive equipment onstage in a mind-boggling display of auto-destruction, The Who hope eventually to drop destruction entirely from their act, as they have already done in Britain.

Roger Daltrey, singer with The Who, explains: "Until we have made a big enough name for ourselves in the States, we will keep the destruction in the act. But we will eventually prefer to concentrate on other sides of our act."

THE WHO Exclusively on DECCA RECORDS

THE WHO DON'T DISAPPOINT FANS BY BREAKING THEIR INSTRUMENTS
. . . it's a fake—most of them can be patched up

Teeny-Boppers Storm Pop Group After Show At The Gardens

y NICK LEES
f The Journal

Police fought with screaming en-agers who tried to scale e Edmonton Gardens stage aturday night after a perform-nce by the English pop group he Who.

The youths climbed over steel arriers in front of the stage nd tried to carry off the pop roup's instruments as sou-enirs.

But the organizers had antici-ated such a scene from the 000 youngsters, and a well-repared plan swung into opera-on.

Police and security guards ormed a line in front of the age and the group's helpers rew back anybody who broke rough.

"Nobody was hurt," said pro-oter Benny Benjamin. "But ere could have been if our ans to counter a rush hadn't one off like clockwork."

ANS SAT DOWN

When The Who first appeared n stage, the fans rushed for-ard. Others stood on their airs and screamed.

Lights were switched on again and it was announced the show would not go on unless the fans sat down. They did.

During the performance, 12 girls fainted amid the heat and hysteria. They were carried to first aid posts.

The object of the fans' atten-tion were four London lads, Roger Daltrey, 23, Pete Town-shend, 22, Keith Moon, 21, and John Entwistle, 23.

They were about 15 minutes late on stage—delayed mainly because the electronic device triggering off the smoke bombs released at the end of their act, did not work.

But once they got going, they worked the fans up into a frenzy.

GOT MONEY'S WORTH

And the fans, who had paid nearly $14,000 at the box office, reckoned they got their money's worth.

Fair-haired lead singer Roger Daltrey, dressed in shocking pink velvet pants and a scarlet velvet jacket, threw the micro-phone into the crowd and then pulled it back like a yo-yo.

Drummer Keith Moon started throwing his drumsticks away over his shoulder—and then, finally his drum. Fortunately, of course, there was somebody behind to catch it.

Pete Townshend, lead guitar, with a white-sequined jacket and frilly collar, jitterbugged round the stage.

Pyschedelic-suit-wearing John Entwistle kept a steady rhythm on the bass.

"I'm sort of the anchor man," he said almost apologetically.

NO DISAPPOINTMENT

For an hour, the group played away and the long-haired fans bobbed their heads in time, bit their fingernails and yelled.

The group, known throughout the world for their last act end-ing when they break their in-struments, did not disappoint the fans.

As the last number got going, the smoke bombs went off, Keith Moon threw away his cymbals and then his drums, and Pete Townshend broke up his guitar.

The fans went wild and tried to rush the stage for souvenirs.

Afterwards, Roger Daltrey said: "We'd have an enormous bill if we really broke all the instruments every act. Most of them can be patched up."

The instrument-breaking act started one night, said Daltrey, when Pete broke his guitar on a low ceiling.

"The fans like it so much we have always kept it in," he said.

Edmonton groups Willie and the Walkers, The Heat, the Warp Factor and the Young Ones, were on the 4½-hour bill.

The Young Ones, all aged between 13 and 14, had been asked to play at the request of The Who.

Said Benny Benjamin: "I reckon the evening was a great success. We're going to have The Who back again next year with more English pop groups."

The Who had to be locked in their bus at the back of the stage for safety before they left the Gardens. Hundreds of autograph hunters and souvenir seekers milled around.

Indian Column Starts Tuesday

heTe

O: Pop music i
of the best thi
ginality actually
the root of the
Keith Moon, the
erything at once
d, the guitarist
ltrey, who sings
rom it—which is
sist around who
ckground is unus
any ambition to
h Horn in school
tivity into pop t
king group in E
n that has had
world. They're a
sh. Don't miss

Who, What, Where and Why

THE TAMPA TIMES, Wednesday, March 20, 1968 5-B

Instrument Smashing Scheduled Here Friday

Who are The Who? Or is it, who IS The Who? One might be tempted to say, who gives a hoot (for phonetic reasons), but a lot of their fans might take exception.

Anyway, The Who is a vocal group which ranks third in the hearts of Englishmen, teen-agers, and mad mods who dig the new sounds in music.

Or so says their public relations representatives out in Beverly Hills, Calif., and on Madison Avenue, which aren't bad addresses for your public relations representatives to have, by the way.

Peter Townshend (now, really, just because he was sent off to the continent by the royal family after failing to win Margaret's hand in matrimony, that is a bit much) Roger Daltrey, Keith Moon and John Entwhistle got their big start by busting up their musical instruments on stage to the accompaniment of shrieks of the girls.

They still go that route in the colonies (meaning the U.S.A.), but have knocked off that kick in England. They will demonstrate their smashing instrument-smashing routine at Curtis Hixon Hall on Friday.

"The Who," say their PR folks, "became bored with the current rock music scene and devised their instrument-smashing routine for concert performances, now one of the most internationally famous (and most copied) in all of popdom."

A narrow little book-marker type flyer tells everyone to "watch them destroy all $35,000 equipment."

That may be a bit of exaggeration, old man, but that is what the pop music business is all about, anyway, so why quibble over a few thousand this way or that.

It's the shrieks from the birds that matter most. They and their teen-aged boy friends are the ones with all the money these days. — BOB MARTIN

THE WHO, from left, Keith Moon, Peter ...nsend, John Entwistle and Roger Daltrey, provide on the spot instrument pulverization in their live performances. (Pop Scene Photo)

...ne Is Wild When Group Plays

Breaking Guitars Costly Antic For 'Who' Group

By MIKE JAHN

...'ve broken 95 guitars," ...r Townshend said. "I ...e six that I really liked. ...as the first to do it and ...n it. I broke the only one I had once."

...eter is the energetic lead ...arist for the Who, a Brit... rock group currently on ... of the United States. He ...on his motel bed, between ... at San Francisco's Fill...e Auditorium, and ex...ned why he's known for ...ting guitars with a cer... disrespect:

...We were playing things ... couldn't be surpassed," he ... "We couldn't play them ... louder or any harder. ...re was nothing else that ... could do."

... began several years ago ...n the Who were playing a ...cert in England. Peter uses ...dback like an ordinary ...n uses an electric toothbrush, swinging the guitar back and forth to bring it close to the amplifier and get the right tone. The guitar began to bang into the amplifier, and then the ceiling. Eventually he began to smash them, and before long the group was ending their concerts by breaking the guitar, throwing the drums around, and disappearing under the cover of a smoke bomb explosion that obliterated view of the stage.

Costly Gimmick

Though guitars can be expensive, Peter has a solidly anti-McLuhanesque view of smashing them. "Love of the instrument shouldn't stand between me and the music," he says. He makes no estimate of the exact cost.

The Who is generally known as an in-person group because the sound of guitars splintering and smoke bombs igniting is hard to capture on record, but they have three albums on Decca, "The Who Sings My Generation," "Happy Jack," and "The Who Sell Out," their latest.

The Who Sell Out is distinguished by an album cover featuring each member of the group shown testing a different brand name product. Peter is shown with a giant tube of deodorant under his arm.

The album is a half-hour segment designed as a radio program for Radio London, the defunct pirate radio station, including commercials and station breaks. It has created only ripples in the placid sea of American top 40 rock stations.

Ignite Audience

But the Who music is excellent. On record, they ignite the audience with excellen... rock songs, with minimal con... concocted effects, and in per...son they blend hardrock ex...huberance with considerabl... gymnastics to turn on an audience.

Keith Moon, the Who 2...year-old drummer, flails th... drums with incredible ener... while gasping for breath li... a beached guppy.

Lead singer Roger Daltr... jumps about stage, twirli... the microphone over his he... and banging it into one ... Keith's two bass drums.

Peter Townshend fl... around the stage taking sp...tacular roundhouse strokes ... his guitar (a movement he ...mits stealing from Roll... Stone Keith Richards).

John Entwistle, the bass... stands to one side and is c...tent to seem quite disinter...ed in the acrobatics going ... to his left. "When we sta... we were quite mad at him... that," Peter says. "We wanted him to get in there and do his thing. But his acting as an anchor is probably the only thing that's kept us together."

Peter admits having been bothered by the fact that American audiences expect him to break guitars, a feature he dropped from the Who's British stage act some time ago, and has even cut down on drastically in this country. But it could be worse.

(Copyright (C) 1968 by Pop Scene Service)
(Distributed by Bell-McClure Syndicate)

'The Who'

...he Who" from England ...perform tonight at Curtis ...n Hall. Tickets are on ... through the box office. ...haps one of the more sig...ant things about this rock ...up, as distinguished from ...ers, is that the band mem...s destroy their equipment ...he end of each show.

Rock Reaches New High With The Who

Wednesday night saw the first Montreal appearance of the Who, an English rock and roll quartet. In the three years that they have been recording the Who have become a major influence on the development of rock music.

The Who originated the use of electronic distortion as a part of contemporary pop music, and they created a blue-based, electrically augmented sound that was a major innovation in the usually eclectic world of rock and roll. Their experimentation with sound led to a stage presentation which climaxes with a wild melee in which their instruments are thrown about the stage and a guitar is ultimately smashed to bits.

The Who ran onto the stage of the Forum, resplendent in clothes of velvet, silk and sequins. They are indeed a spectacular group to watch. They play so long and loud that one's head begins to ring, wondering where all the sounds are coming from. And all the time they move about and attack their instruments with a satisfying violence. Keith Moon, the drummer, leans forward with his arms flying, crashing his sticks down on drums and cymbals, sustaining a rhythmic pattern which is unmatched by any other rock drummer. Peter Townshend, the guitarist and leader, is tall and overpoweringly elegant, as he flails his guitar with great circular sweeps of his outstretched arm. John Entwhistle stands unmoving through everything and plays a solid bass line, while vocalist Roger Daltrey hits things with his microphone, prances around the stage, kneels penitentially before the drums, and sings.

The compositions, mostly by Townshend, are characterized by an unrelenting drive created by the drums, bass and guitar, over which the lead vocals and harmonies soar. The lyrics are marvellously unpretentious. They are not quite the normal love songs nor are they incomprehensible poetry. Often they are humorous narratives, as is the case with Townshend's mini-opera, A Quick One. The composition is in five distinct parts, and tells the tale of a girl whose lover is away, and she, in loneliness, is a little unfaithful. In the end she is forgiven. The singing begins with an a capella bass trio, and ends with a lengthy rococco rendition of the single line "you are forgiven" sung falsetto.

The Who create an atmosphere, not of potentially explosive excitement for which the Beatles or Rolling Stones are famous, but rather one of awe. The crowd at the Forum sat almost impassive as they were bombarded by the deafeningly loud sounds from the stage and the Who's frenetic actions. Only a few times when the Forum guards became hostile was the spell broken, but for the most part even those guards unclenched their fists and watched.

In the end the Who sang their modern classic My Generation, and fulfilling their image, and broke things up. While the bass continued to beat out a steady rhythm, drums began to roll about and Daltrey ran around swinging and striking his microphone. Townshend extracted an amazing variety of sounds from his guitar and amplifier, threw it in the air, caught it, pushed it aside and then smashed another one.

The sacrifice had been made, and everyone went home happy.

DANE LANKEN

This and preceding pages: A sampling of memorabilia and press coverage from the Who's 1967 and '68 American tours.

03: 1968
MAGIC BUS

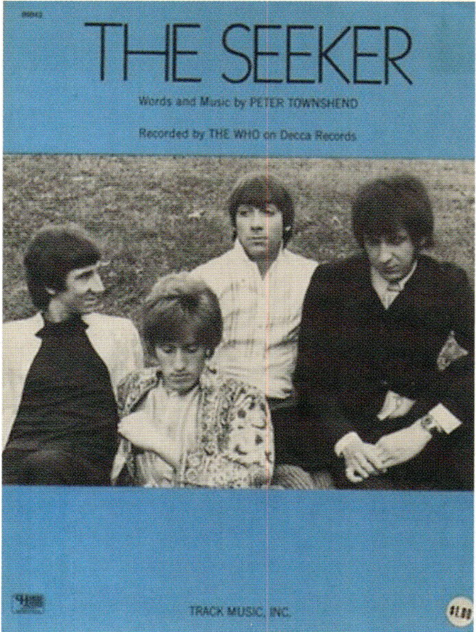

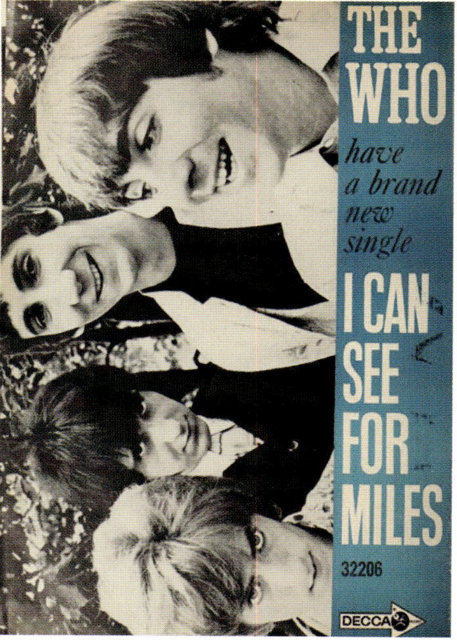

Examples of how Tom's Who photographs were used over the years for sheet music, magazine colour pin-ups, album covers (opposite, top right) and tour programmes for the group's spring 1968 US tour (above) and Australasian tour (opposite, bottom left).

The Who went through a transition in 1968. In England, newer acts like Cream, the Jimi Hendrix Experience, Traffic and Pink Floyd had come to the fore, appealing to underground audiences as well as achieving commercial success in the pop charts. Pete had kept back 'I Can See For Miles' as an 'ace in the hole' should the Who need it, and when the single was released in October 1967, despite being a Top 10 hit in America, it only reached 13 on the *NME* chart. "It was the ultimate Who record," Pete later reflected, "yet it didn't sell." Its failure could be put into context in relation to the changing British pop scene. The pioneering pirate stations – the Who's greatest ally – had been outlawed by the government in August, and the charts were engulfed by balladeers like Engelbert Humperdinck, Frankie Vaughan and Tom Jones.

PETE TOWNSHEND: Also, I think London had been overtaken, not just by hippie outfits like Pink Floyd and Soft Machine, and the Jimi Hendrix-inspired outfits, but also by the *International Times* and *Oz* magazine crowd – that cool, lefty kind of thinking.

The Who Sell Out, an inventive album arranged (in part) like a non-stop Radio London show, was released in December 1967, but could climb no higher than 12 on the *NME* LP chart and 48 on *Billboard*.

With the rising debt incurred from the previous three years hovering over the Who, live work was their only recourse. Premier Talent booked them into a punishing six-week coast-to-coast itinerary across America and Canada in the spring, and a further nine weeks over the summer.

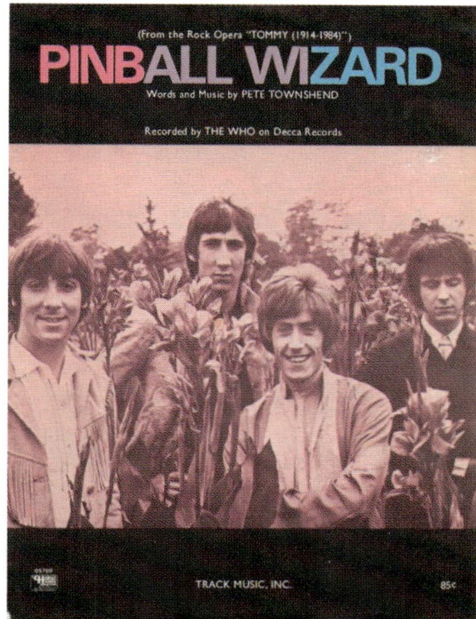

After the Herman's Hermits tour the previous year, Tom Wright had moved to New York City, sharing a loft apartment on Houston St. with Geoff Daking, drummer for the Blues Magoos (Wright photographed the sleeve for their third album, *Basic Blues Magoos*). There had been efforts to bring Tom back to London to work for the Who's organisation, but his drug bust was an impediment.

In January 1968, Chris Stamp contacted Tom about going on the road again as the Who's production manager over the gruelling weeks ahead. "As their road manager and friend, my feeling was 'Maybe these guys can't make it in America'," Wright recalled in 2006, "because normally when the Who would play and come to the end of their set and break up their guitars, people were just stunned. They didn't know whether to clap or run away or anything."

Tom recruited his young cousin Chris Laumer to assist.

CHRIS LAUMER: I was kicked out of school in Dade City, Florida because of my long hair. Then Tom called out of the blue and wanted to know if I would be an equipment man on tour for the Who. It was a shock, but I was ready to get out of town, so a week later I flew to New York to meet Tom. We then went to meet up with the Who. I travelled on the rented bus with Tom, Bob Pridden – who was my boss – Jonesy the driver and the Who. Sometimes the band flew but otherwise they travelled in the bus. All the equipment was packed on there and my job was to take care of it. I got paid 90 bucks a week, which seemed like a lot to a 17-year-old in return for an adventure of a lifetime.

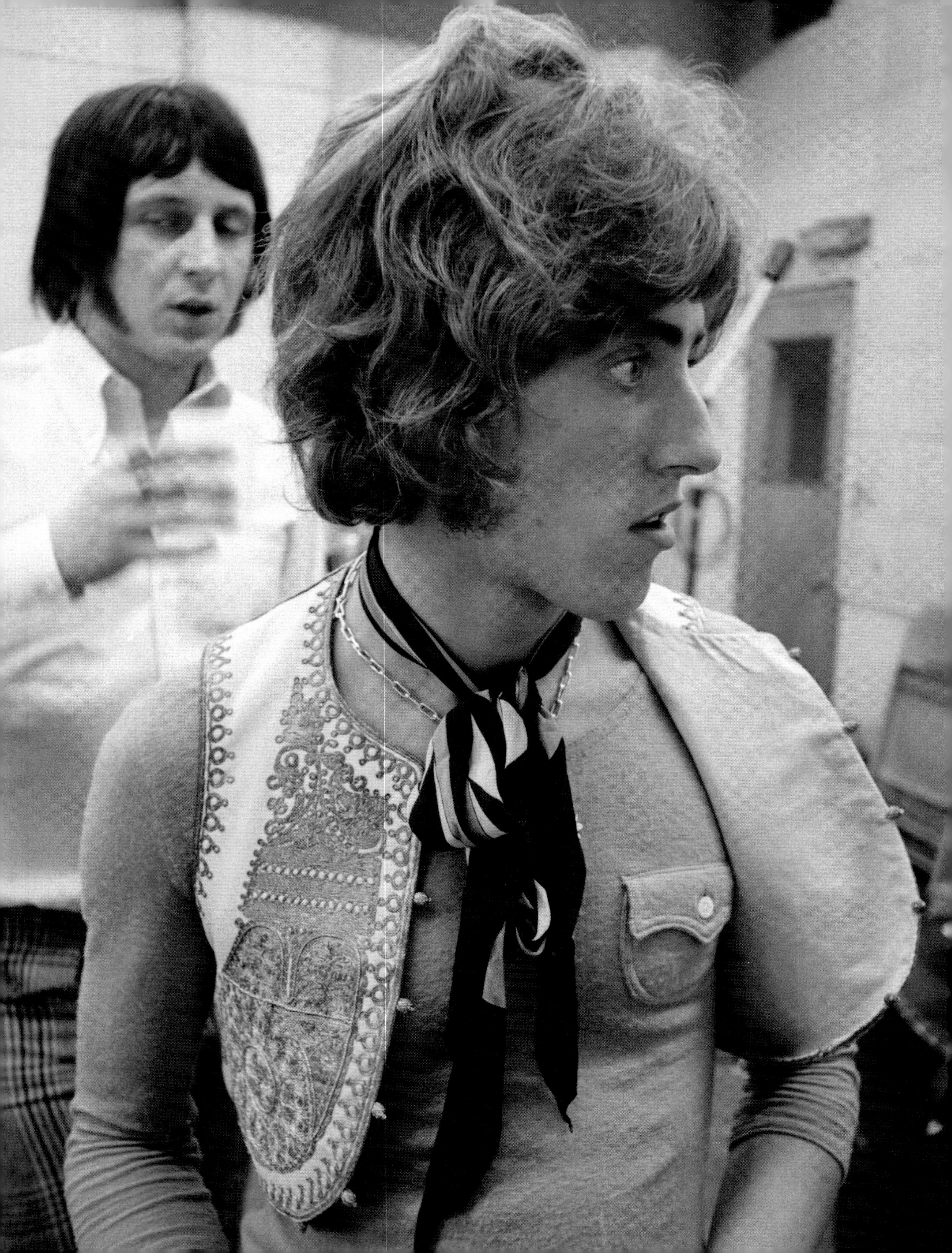

Waiting to go onstage, unknown location, US tour, spring 1968

The Who's first tour of America as a headlining act started on the West Coast. In Los Angeles, members of the Who attended Richie Havens' show at the Troubadour. In the crowd Keith met Jeannie Franklyn (aka Genie the Tailor), a well-known scenester and clothes designer, who was holding a metallic red, white and blue striped coat. She invited him to try it on. Moon cajoled her into parting with the jacket, which he wore throughout the tour. (Sadly, Franklyn passed away the following year in a tragic motor accident involving the British folk-rock band Fairport Convention.)

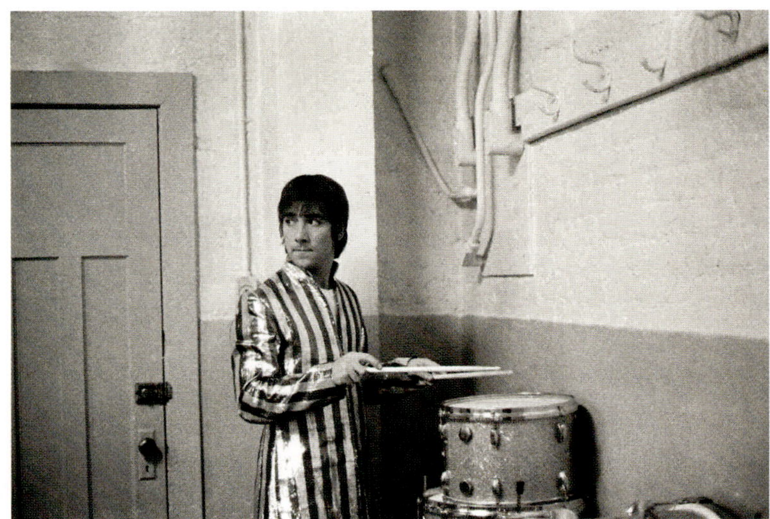

Filming the 'Call Me Lightning' promo in Hollywood, CA, February 25 (or 26), 1968

Surprisingly, there were no concerts scheduled in LA; while in town, the band relaxed, did press and photo sessions, and completed a new single, 'Call Me Lightning', with Kit Lambert at Gold Star Studios. To help promote the record, the group shot a promotional film in an empty warehouse. "It looked very much like the factory used in the closing scenes of *The Ipcress File*," Pete wrote in a contemporary report for *NME*. Various props like tin helmets, explosive devices and walkie-talkies were deployed, and Keith played the starring role of a humanoid wind-up toy, to which the others gave chase.

PETE TOWNSHEND: That was organised by Decca. I remember at the time just thinking this is a complete and utter waste of time. Good fun, though.

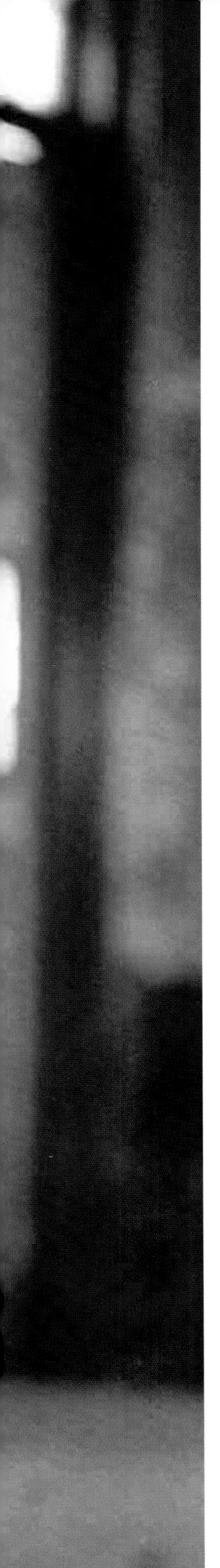

Opera House, Exposition Gardens, Peoria, IL, March 10, 1968

The early Who were a supreme visual act but, unfortunately, few of their pre-*Tommy* stage performances were professionally filmed. An exception was when a BBC documentary crew, headed by director Tony Palmer, filmed the band on their tour bus as they crisscrossed America's highways in spring 1968, as well as the show at the Peoria Opera House, Illinois. In his interview for Palmer's *All My Loving*, Pete stated that the Who's intention was "to play out all the adrenalin and all the aggression, and show the audience that you are a frustrated character, that you do want to get something out of your system, and you do want to do it in front of them". Wright's pictures show the cameraman and film arc lights set up to capture the action. At the end of 'My Generation', Tom can be seen leaping on stage, camera in hand, after the band had left the stage, assisting Bob Pridden in preventing over-eager audience members from taking a broken guitar or drum as a souvenir.

PETE TOWNSHEND: On the bus, you couldn't get away from Keith. Socially, I enjoyed hanging out with him – he was good fun, he was funny, he always made me laugh. This was the early days of my interest in [Indian guru] Meher Baba, trying to meditate and fast, which I didn't do very successfully. My girlfriend Karen was there sometimes; she came to stay with me when we had a few breaks on the tour.

This was also the last tour on which I smoked marijuana. I smoked it occasionally – couldn't always get it – but when I could, I smoked it. At the start of the tour in San Francisco, I met [Baba devotee] Rick Chapman, who told me that Meher Baba had prescribed against the use of hallucinogenics, and he said that cannabis did have hallucinogenic properties, so I stopped smoking it.

Florida, March 18–24, 1968

After shows in Texas, the Who had a week off, so they accepted Tom's invitation to relax and unwind at his stepfather's property in Florida. The weariness of the long days on the road can be detected in Pete, John and Roger's faces, while the chance for mischief and mayhem is clearly evident on Keith's.

CHRIS LAUMER: I lived with my folks in a little town called Lacoochee. The Who were interested in checking out the river where I'd lived my entire life. We went to town and bought 22 calibre rifles to shoot beer cans by the river, and we saw alligators, turtles and snakes. Keith was trying to kill a beer can when his gun jammed. He got pissed off and to my amazement threw the rifle into the water.

SABRINA LAUMER [Tom's half-sister]: Tom, who was 13 years older than me, came for a rare visit, bringing John Entwistle, Pete Townshend and Keith Moon. He picked me up after school in my dad's Cadillac and these rock'n'roll legends in the car with him. I was an awkward, shy 11-year-old and remember cringing in the back seat, terrified, as Tom drove 100 miles an hour on the long drive home.

I headed for the lake to calm down and be in nature, as I loved the serenity of the water. I had not stopped to change clothes from school and was wearing a red dress as I tromped through the cat tails that lined the lake bank. I heard shots fired as I was walking on the other side of the lake from our house. I was trained to use a rifle myself and often shot rattlesnakes, so I was not alarmed until I saw Keith Moon in front of our house, aiming and shooting at me. I assumed he thought I was an exotic bird. Being unwise and foolish, my reaction was to act casual and not show fear.

When I returned home, I sequestered myself in my room, but not before my dad angrily asked if Keith had shot at me, which I affirmed. As I cringed in my room, someone knocked on the door and entered. It was Keith with a playful smile, saying with a flourish 'Cabaña room service', a tea towel over his arm and presenting me with a dinner tray. My guess is that my dad had a talk with him and this was Keith's way of making amends.

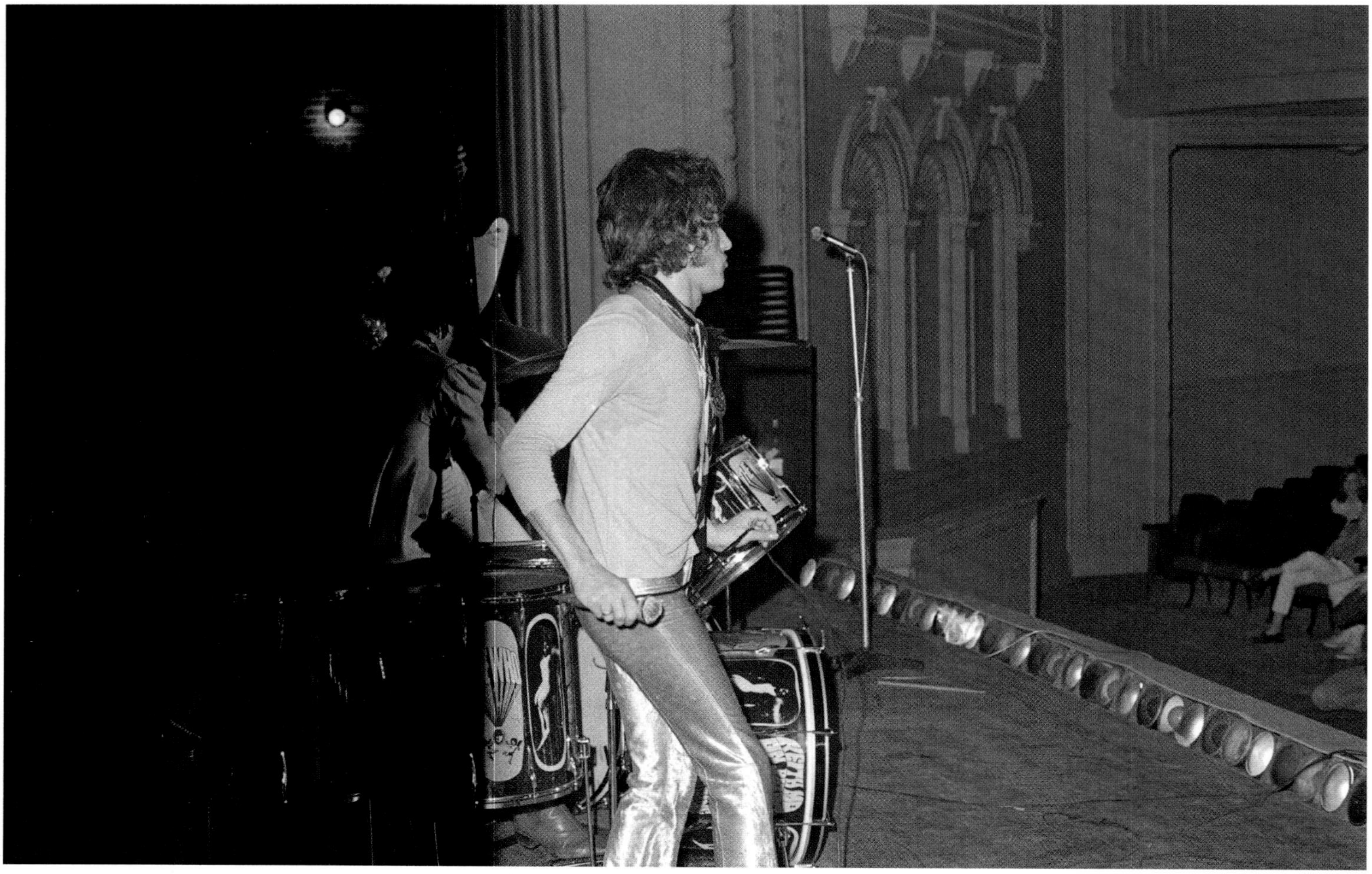

Pete playing a Gibson 345 Stereo on stage, The Forum, Montreal, Canada, March 27, 1968

PETE TOWNSHEND: I played whatever I could get my hands on. I didn't have a preference for any guitar. I never have. When I see photos of old Gibsons that now sell for $600,000, I just think it's a fucking chunk of wood. That's how I feel about it. I didn't have any kind of real attachment to the guitars.

Westbury Music Fair, Long Island, NY, March 30, 1968

Bob Pridden looks apprehensive while setting up the band's gear at this 3,000-seat capacity indoor venue designed around a circular, rotating stage. The support bill featured a Boston group called Orpheus. According to showbiz bible *Variety*, promoter Lee Gruber paid the Who $10,000 for their appearance – an indicator of how their American concert fees were slowly creeping up.

Premier
THE WHO
Premier

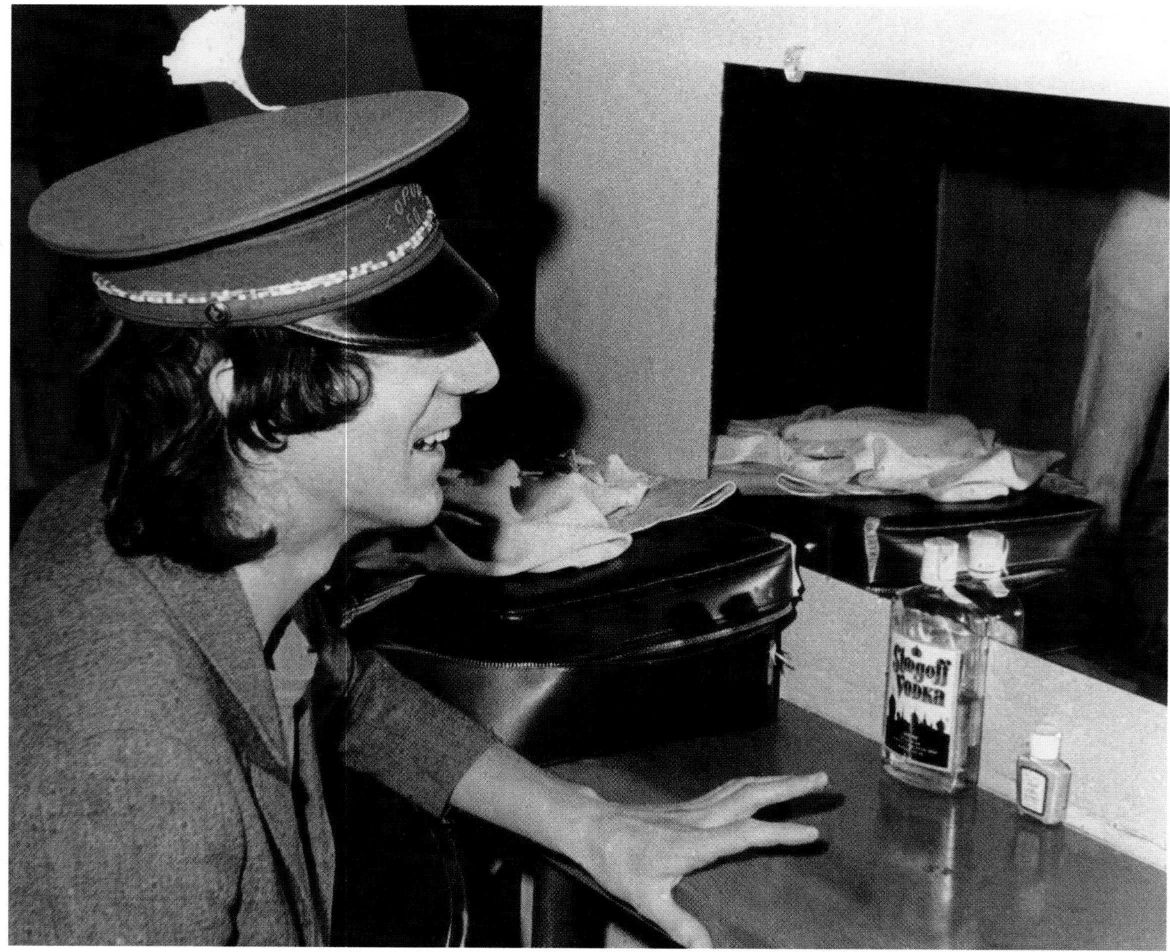
Smirnoff
Vodka

Premier
THE WHO
Premier

Premier
THE WHO
Premier

Premier
THE WHO
Premier

Premier
THE WHO
Premier

Premier
THE WHO
Premier

FOR
SALE

FOR
SALE

Pete with girlfriend Karen Astley, somewhere in America, April 1968

As the long US tour of spring '68 wound to a close, Pete's girlfriend Karen Astley flew out to be with him for the final leg. During a gas stop, the couple investigated a yard with cars for sale, including several vintage Cadillacs.

PETE TOWNSHEND: I was looking for an old Lincoln all the time. I did buy one in San Francisco on one of our early tours, but then Chris Stamp arrived and took all of the tour money to pay a tax bill, so I had to cancel the sale.

I felt very lonely in this period, and what sustained me was the love affair with Karen. She was so pretty and so lovely and so fantastic and she came to New York for some periods and then subsequently, very soon after, we got married [on May 20, 1968 – the day after Pete's 23rd birthday]. She was absolutely the love of my life and sustained me, made me feel that I didn't have to chase after girls on the road. The other thing that sustained me was my interest in Meher Baba, which became something, and also Sufism, Sufi writing and stuff like that.

Afternoon rehearsal, Fillmore East, NYC, April 5, 1968

The Who's stay in New York was overshadowed by the death of Martin Luther King on April 4, and punctuated by Keith Moon's destructive antics, resulting in the band being evicted from three city hotels. The Who were originally booked to play two shows per night at Bill Graham's Fillmore East venue in the East Village, on April 5 and 6, but due to pressure from City Ordinance officials, the four concerts were condensed into one per night. During the afternoon, the band rehearsed in the empty theatre.

PETE TOWNSHEND: I'm playing a Danelectro Coral Hornet here [overleaf]. I started to play them because they were really cheap guitars, so I could smash them without worrying too much, but they wouldn't feed back at all. I always needed feedback so I liked guitars that were semi-acoustic, like Rickenbackers, which is where feedback began for me. Part of my sound is that kind of Birdman thing, which is huge, Marshall-driven, but Danelectros had an amazing, beautiful clean sound, which I really liked.

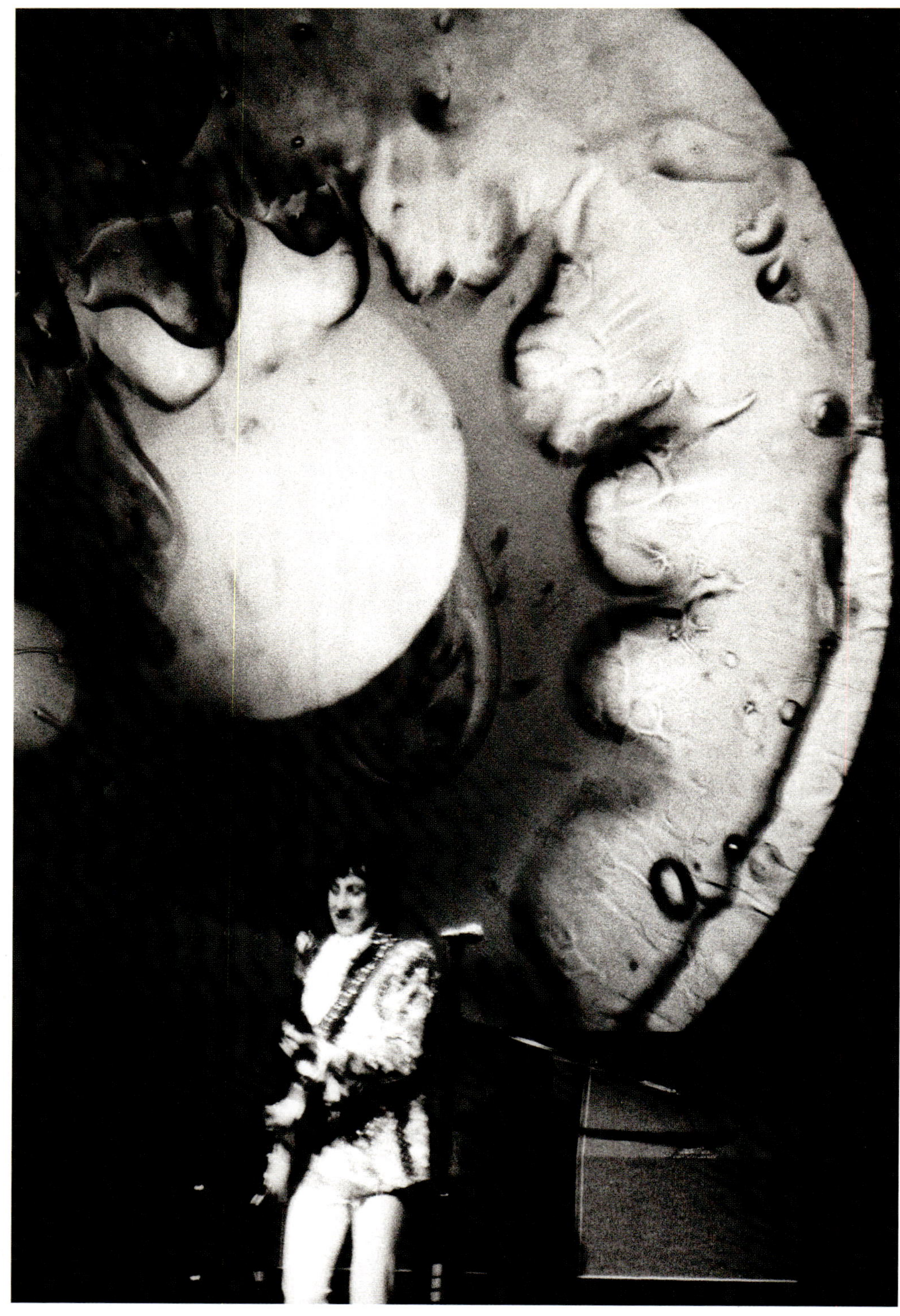

Fillmore East, NYC, April 5, 1968

As well as the rehearsal, Tom's camera captured the first night's performance with the in-house Joshua Light Show behind them. This was the last time Pete wore his trademark sparkly glittering coat, designed by his girlfriend Karen, which had been a striking visual component of the Who's shows over the past nine months. Both Fillmore concerts were recorded for a stillborn live album, which was eventually released 50 years later in 2018.

PETE TOWNSHEND: The interesting thing about the Fillmore concerts to me is some of the artists we played with. I remember [jazz saxophonist] Cannonball Adderley supporting, and he was just fantastic. The guys in his band were not quite as bemused by us as he was, but he was so positive and encouraging, a fabulous fellow.

Following the Who's spring tour of the States, Tom moved into an apartment at the Albert Hotel in New York – his business card stating: 'Tom Wright Alive and Well Living in the Albert Hotel'. The Who came back in the summer for a further nine-week sweep across America, but Tom did not go with them this time. Prior to the trip, in an interview with British music paper *Disc*, Pete revealed it could be their last Stateside tour. "It's alright on stage and the audiences are quite incredible. But you just keep slogging away, travelling the highways and the freeways and the byways and the airways... You can't work, you can't think – your mind's blanked out."

When the tour reached New York, Tom and his cameras accompanied the band to a memorable show co-headlined by the Doors at the Singer Bowl in Queens, before a near sell-out audience of 16,000. (The support was a Boston band called Kangaroo for whose only album Tom photographed the sleeve.)

Chris Stamp at Premier Talent office, NYC, August 2, 1968

Chris Stamp was the younger brother of film star Terence. In 1967, after three years of co-managing the Who, he and partner Kit Lambert used what experience they'd gained from the music business to set up Track Records, signing the Who, the Jimi Hendrix Experience and the Crazy World of Arthur Brown, among others.

During this period, Stamp spent most of his time in New York, whipping up the Who's American promotional campaign in the same office on 200 West 57th St. as Premier Talent, the band's US agents.

After Lambert and Stamp were dismissed as the Who's managers in 1975, Stamp remained on good terms with the band members until his death in 2012.

Pete on his way to the Singer Bowl, NYC, August 2, 1968

Performing in sticky humidity on a circular, revolving stage, the Who closed the first half of the show with their demolition finale (the Doors came on after the break and filled the second half). However, a long delay between acts and Jim Morrison's theatrics incited the crowd to riot. A girl was injured in the melee, the incident inspiring Pete to write 'Sally Simpson' for *Tommy*.

PETE TOWNSHEND: When we played with the Doors in New York, one of their fans jumped on stage to touch Jim Morrison's face and was thrown back into the crowd by a security guy and cut her face. I spent an hour with Jim after that show. I remember saying, 'You really need to go and see that girl, the guards smashed her up.' She was bleeding, and Jim and I both consoled her. It stuck in my mind as an image.

SOUND CITY

PETE TOWNSHEND: Roger's hair is starting to grow into its natural curly state. During the early days of the Who, he used to straighten his hair – that's why [Who roadie] Bob Pridden called him 'Dip' for Dippity-do. By the time we came back to America to play *Tommy*, Roger had that full Seventies rock god look – bare chest, tasselled outfits and a large mane.

Pages 150-155: The Who in full flight at the Singer Bowl.

Overleaf (bottom left): Bob Pridden provides back-up vocals on 'Magic Bus', the Who's current single in America.

04: 1969 LISTENING TO YOU

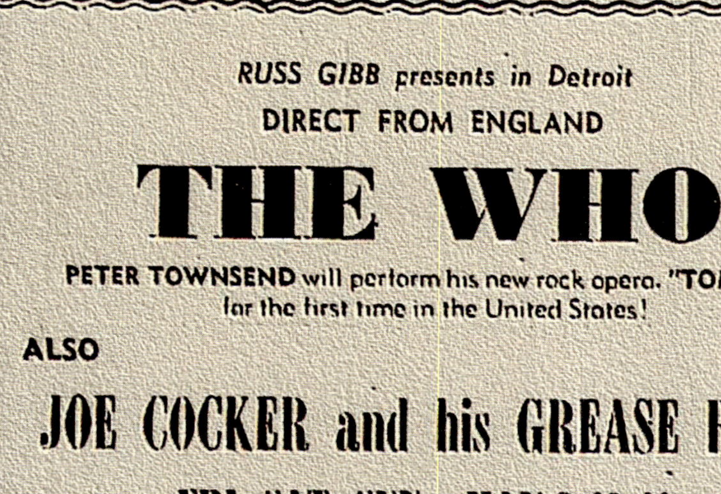

Left: Original advertisement and (opposite) flyer for the Who's three-night run at the Grande Ballroom, Detroit, May 1969.

PETE TOWNSHEND: It was great to play the Grande. That was a really great gig, a great crowd. I actually stayed with Tom inside the place. I remember I spent the night in his room, just eating tuna out of a can and roller-skating around the empty ballroom floor with music blaring over the PA. It was fabulous.

On Saturday, March 9, 1968, the Who played Detroit's main 'underground' venue, the Grande Ballroom – located in the Petoskey-Otsego neighbourhood – for the first time. The Grande was one of several major dance venues built in Detroit in the late Twenties, and was a centre of elegance, before the area declined. The building got taken over in 1966 by Russ Gibb, a local high school teacher and part-time DJ, with the intention of turning it into an alternative music venue along the lines of what he'd seen in other parts of America.

"When I walked into the Grande for the first time with the Who," Tom said in 2006, "it was during a long, depressing tour in which the band's attitude was 'After this tour, we'll play England and Europe, but we're never coming back to America.' Under those circumstances, after driving through the ghetto to some place that looked like it ought to be condemned. we walked reluctantly through the front door, with the band going, 'Let's do 45 minutes and run.' From the first two or three notes on stage, the way it sounded and the intensity of the audience, the Grande changed the Who's whole career path."

Along with the band, Tom was blown away by the acoustics and atmosphere in the second-floor hardwood-floor ballroom. The Grande made such an impact on him that he relinquished his post as the Who's US tour production manager, and relocated from New York to the Motor City in late 1968. He took over management of the venue, living and working in the building with a hand-picked team to maintain the building in time for shows each weekend.

"The Grande Ballroom was one of – if not *the* – most acoustically perfect building that I'd ever been in," Wright said. "It was not terribly big by Detroit standards, but acoustically, it was the Stradivarius of buildings. The English bands would come in, expecting the same old thing, and they would set up on stage and do a soundcheck and suddenly they realised the building was working with them rather than against them."

With *Tommy* – much of it written while on the road the previous year – about to be released in America, the Who chose to debut the rock opera at the Grande during a three-night stand that broke previous attendance records at the venue. As well as taking pictures of the rehearsal and shows, Tom also recorded the opening night on his portable tape recorder, preserving an important moment in the Who's career.

RUSS GIBB PRESENTS FROM ENGLAND
WHO
MAY 9-10-11
Joe Cocker and his Grease Band
MAEND
FRIDAY
CARL LUNDGREN
SATURDAY
MIXED GENERATION
RUSS
SUN
GRANDE BALLROOM
Detroit Grand River at Beverly one block south of Joy 8 30 pm You must be 17 Phone 834 4904 or 834 9348 Adv Tickets Grinnell's Hudson's, House of Mystique Mixed Media Chumley's 124
W Gd River E Lansing Discount Records Friday, Saturday
Limit on Sunday

Pete at station WKNR-FM, Detroit, MI, with DJ Russ Gibb, May 9, 1969

PETE TOWNSHEND: I remember Russ fondly. I went and did a long interview with him. He was a real supporter of the band and he was a proper theatre manager. He knew what to do; it wasn't just about the Who – everybody who played the Grande was really carefully selected. He was a very special character.

Listening to FM stations was always a joy, particularly after 11 o'clock because the DJs were given free rein, so they would mix the LA music and the San Francisco bands and the Beatles, the Stones, the Who and the Kinks etc., but they would also play jazz artists, they would play string quartets, they would play whatever they wanted to play, so it was a real trip, a real journey through a whole load of musical styles. Every station had its own fingerprint, its own stamp, so the enthusiasms of the individual DJs would be the things that actually gave the stations their vibe, and they often ran in tandem with an AM station which would be in the same building, which just played pop all day. The thing about the FM stations is that they were sustained by the AM stations which got advertising, but the FM stations at that time didn't get advertising, so there were no commercials, there were no stops, there were no pauses, it was just endless music and occasionally interviews. It was a really pure music form.

AMPEX

Grande Ballroom, Detroit, MI, May 9, 1969

PETE TOWNSHEND: The guitar I think I really developed my sound with the most was the Gibson SG, the smaller one with P90 pickups, because when you turn the pickups down, the sound becomes very bright and acoustic sounding; when you turn it up, it gets fuzzy, so that suited me. For example, when I played *Tommy*, there were lots of sections where I would need a very bright sound, but if you grab something like an old Les Paul, it's just grunge. Doesn't matter where you put the controls, it's just grunge.

PETE TOWNSHEND: One of the things I've always said about Keith was that he was never exactly my cup of tea as a studio drummer; he was really fucking difficult to work with a lot of the time because he was always elaborating and decorating too much.

I was processing how to channel my guitar playing. I hadn't fucking learned to play, you know, I'd just played chords. I'd never practised, I'd never done scales. I put all my energy into songwriting and into recording. I suddenly wanted to learn to play and make something out of the sound, but whenever I tried to play a solo, I realised there was a big empty hole because we didn't have a rhythm player.

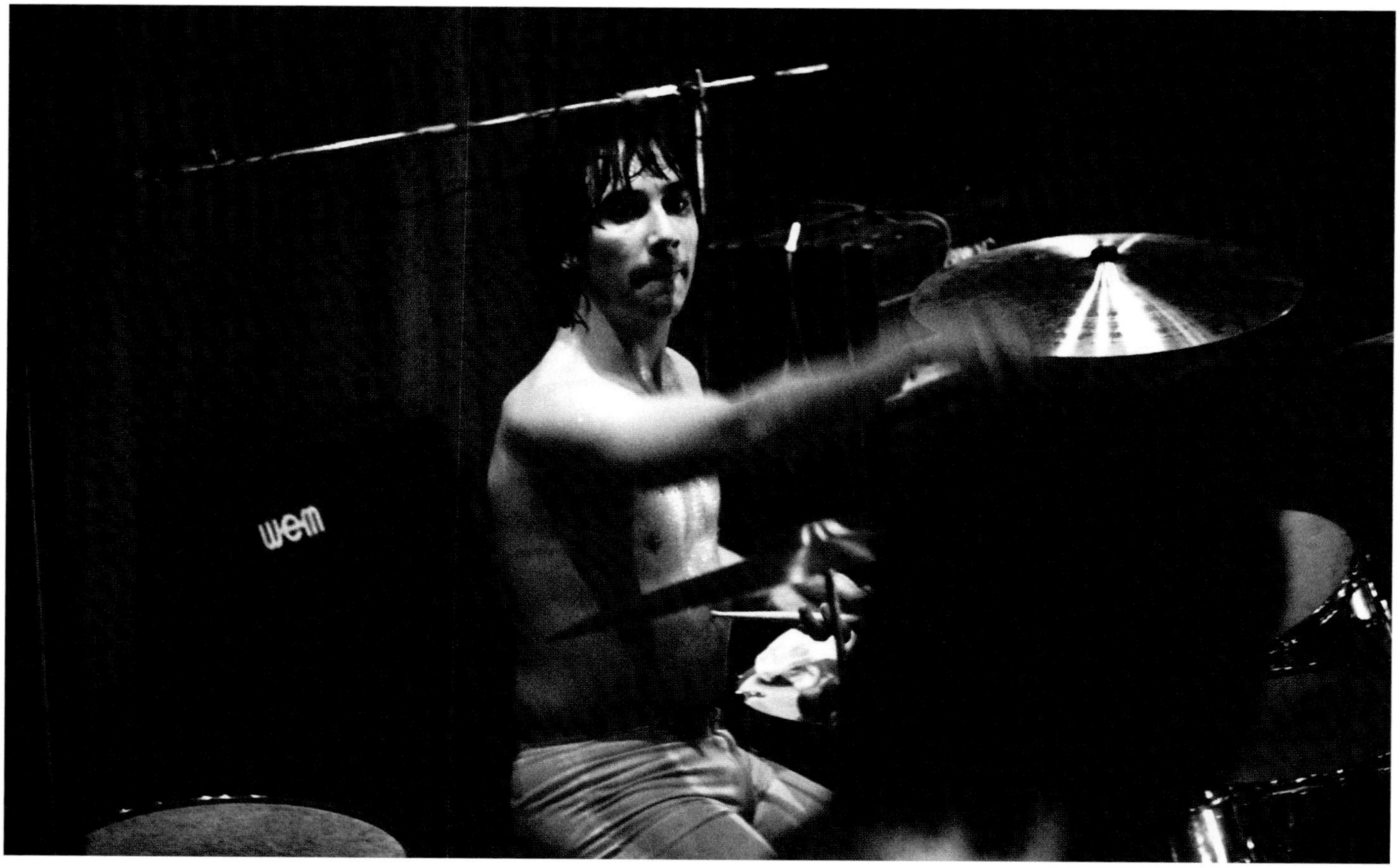

PETE TOWNSHEND: This is what I used to do [opposite]: I'd get on my knees and start noodling around, then start with a riff, then get up and by that time, John would know what the key was, what the tempo was gonna be – he was a true listening musician. Both Keith and John were exceptionally good at listening, so when I was trying to extemporise on the stage and make stuff up on the spur of the moment, I felt like I had this extra engine attached to my guitar, which was quite extraordinary.

The Who's Grande performances in May 1969 marked the start of the real turnaround in the Who's Stateside popularity – and their popularity in general. At last, after two years of scuffling and long tours, there was light at the end of the tunnel. The band played two long US tours that year, including a watershed performance at the Woodstock festival in August, which became a high point of the movie documentary released the following year. As a result, *Tommy* re-entered the charts and continued to sell in vast numbers, as did *Live At Leeds*, which perfectly captured the Who's live attack. By the time they returned to America in June 1970, the Who were newly minted bona fide rock superstars.

EPILOGUE

As the Sixties turned into the Seventies, Tom was still living in Detroit. As well as being responsible for the Grande Ballroom, and providing the album sleeve photography for such Detroit acts as SRC and the Rationals, he was instrumental in stage managing the First Annual Detroit Rock And Roll Revival in 1969, and the Goose Lake International Music Festival in Jackson, Michigan a year later. As he recalled in 2006, "The day after Goose Lake the *Detroit News* printed the schedule and they said at the end of the day, it ended seven minutes *ahead* of schedule and everything went off like clockwork. To me that was like getting the Purple Heart."

Burnt out from his time in Detroit, Tom then worked for the James Gang (featuring Joe Walsh) in Ohio, photographing the sleeve for 1970's *James Gang Rides Again*. Throughout the Seventies and into the Nineties Tom lead a peripatetic lifestyle. In 1971 he and his team of aides known as the Hard Corp – including lifelong friends Patrick Cullie, Royden 'Chuch' Magee and Russ Schlagbaum – caught a freighter over to Europe. Cullie, Magee and Schlagbaum ended up working for the Eagles, the Faces and the Rolling Stones.

In the Seventies, with a short-lived marriage behind him and the birth of his son Tim, Tom taught photography at the Southwest School of Art and Craft in San Antonio, Texas, and later wound up in Austin, freelancing as a photographer and touring with the Eagles, J.D. Souther, Elvis Costello and the Attractions, the Fabulous Thunderbirds, and the Rolling Stones. While living in Texas and also Mexico, struggling with alcohol and depression while in and out of rehab, he would periodically reconnect with his old friend Pete Townshend – particularly on the Who's 1982 and '89 US tours.

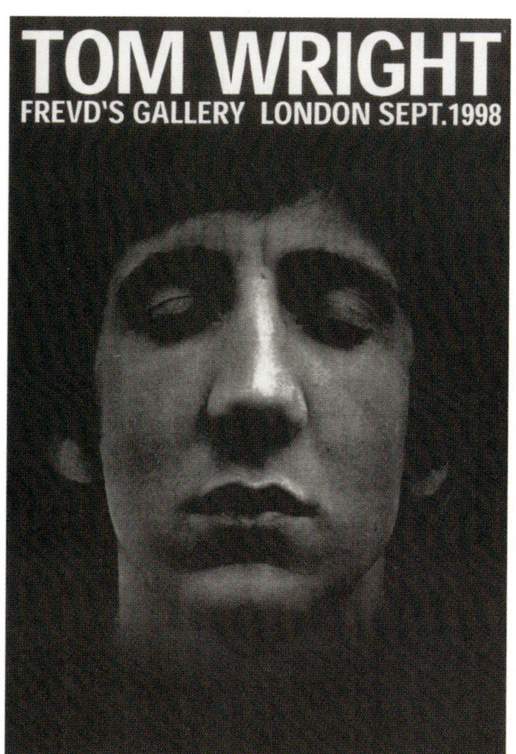

Above: Tom at the International Debut Dennos Museum Center, Traverse, Michigan, November 13, 2003. Opposite: Reconnecting with old friends - getting a trim from Roger in Nyon (Switzerland, 2006) and with Pete in Richmond that same year.

PETE TOWNSHEND: I really enjoyed hanging out with Tom when I got the chance, but he was always quite busy, off doing something. He had a son who he spent a lot of time with, and his mother. There was a lot going on with him; it was complicated and he was often moving. I don't think he ever introduced me to a woman who he regarded as his partner, so it just seemed that he lacked centre, and he was always troubled by the fact that he couldn't organise his own archives. He was somebody who loved to take photographs but didn't want the responsibility of editing and curating them.

In December 1993, Wright's collection of hundreds of thousands of negatives and prints was acquired by the Briscoe Center for American History at the University of Texas in Austin for preservation. He would periodically display key images from the archive of the bands with whom he had worked at enthusiastically greeted exhibitions in the US and London. Tom had been planning a book of his photos and on-the-road war stories for some time. After many false starts, this eventually emerged in 2007 as *Roadwork: Rock & Roll Turned Inside Out* (UK title: *Raising Hell On The Rock 'n' Roll Highway*).

Tom suffered a heart attack and underwent heart bypass surgery in 2005, and in January 2015, a month after losing his dear friend Ian 'Mac' McLagan of the Faces, he suffered a serious stroke. He saw out his days in Michigan until his passing on July 29, 2022.

"[My] pictures are like bricks in a wall," he told *Texas Monthly* when his autobiography was published. "I don't have a favourite brick. I wore my camera as if it were a cross between a gun and a notebook: things and places flew by at warp speed, and I tried to take visual notes so as not to forget."

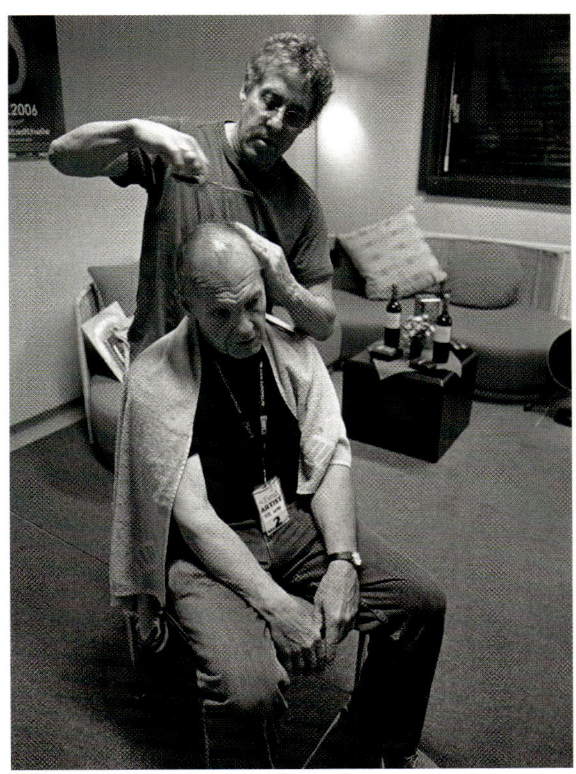

ACKNOWLEDGEMENTS

We'd like to thank:

Tom's family and friends, who continue to care so much about Tom's wonderful photographs, the stories they tell and his legacy: namely, Tom's grandson Anthony Wright, the guardian of Tom's archive; Tom's dear sister Antoinette (Tony) Sales and her husband Dez for their love and belief in Tom and all he did; his sister Sabrina Laumer, who along with Tony were there in 1967 when Tom and Pete reunited; his longtime friend and collaborator Larry Lawrence; his caregiver and travel 'partner in crime' Chris Easter; his old friend from the days at the Grande in Detroit, Gerry Snyder, for his help in identifying the venues in Tom's photos and locating some missing images.

In addition: Russ Millet who believed in Tom's photos and helped preserve them by scanning his work. Brad Mindich and the team at Inveniem for their early support. Chris Flannery for bringing it across the finish line. Nicola Joss for her assistance, Dr Don Carleton and the team at the Briscoe Center at University of Texas, Austin, for their aid and preservation of Tom's archive, and Brad Auerbach who kickstarted the project when Pete Townshend told him decades ago: "The respect you can keep for the Pope, it's your heart I'm after." Brad would like to thank his mom who insisted he wear earplugs the first time he saw the Who, allowing him to enjoy all their subsequent concerts.

Andy Neill would like to thank Richard 'Barney' Barnes (for laying out the carpet and braving 'the Loft From Hell'), Richard Evans, Phil Smee, Mark Lewisohn, Chris Charlesworth, Matt Kent and Dr Jonathan Oates at Ealing Local History.

For their memories: Tim Bartlett, Richard Barnes, Antoinette Sales, Sabrina Laumer and Chris Laumer.

Special thanks to Pete Townshend for sparing an afternoon in his busy schedule in order to look back.

Lucy Beevor and Judith Forshaw for editing and proofreading.

For more examples of Tom Wright's work please check out:
Instagram - @twphoto
Web: https://tomwrightphoto.myportfolio.com

All photos from the Tom Wright Photograph Collection, The Dolph Briscoe Center for American History, The University of Texas at Austin except where stated

KODAK SAFETY FILM

→15A →20 →20A →21 →21A →22

KODAK TRI X PAN FILM

KODAK SAFETY FILM

KODAK TRI X PAN FILM

KODAK TRI X PAN FILM

40 39 38 37 36